Play Piano in
a Flash . . . for Kids!

Play Piano in a Flash . . . for Kids!

Scott Houston

with Susan Stone Tidrow

New York

Contents

PREFACE

Since you have just purchased *Play Piano in a Flash . . . for Kids,* you must know a child who has expressed an interest in learning how to play the piano or keyboard. To tell you the truth, that description would fit almost every child! Most children seem to have an innate curiosity about how to play musical instruments, particularly the piano, simply because it is the instrument most commonly found in homes, schools, and churches.

Your decision to assist the child in your life in learning how to have fun playing the piano is a very wise one. Did you know that the study of music can help children improve and succeed in other areas of learning? An education in the arts engages a wide variety of children's learning styles and increases learning potential for students.

You're probably thinking that this sounds like a commercial for music education . . . and you're absolutely right, it is! Please read on for the scientific proof . . .

- Studies have shown that early and ongoing musical training helps to organize and develop children's brains.
- Two research projects have found that piano instruction in particular can dramatically enhance children's spatial-temporal reasoning skills. These are the skills crucial for greater success in subjects like math and science!
- It is a known fact that students who study music and the other fine arts score higher on the verbal and math portions of the Scholastic Aptitude Test (SAT), a national achievement test, than students with no course work or experience in the arts. Of course, we all know how important SAT scores are in the quest for entrance into the college of your choice.

By now, we hope that you are thinking, "Wow, not only will learning how to play the piano be fun for the child in my life, but it will also be good for him or her!"

Another important benefit from learning to play the piano is that it will help your child to develop a literacy skill needed for a person to be considered literate and educated in the twenty-first century. We are talking about the skill of self-direction.

Self-direction is defined as the ability to set goals, plan for achievement, independently manage time and effort, and independently improve the quality of one's learning and any products that result from the learning experience.

Whew, sounds heavy, doesn't it? But what better skill could you encourage in your child than one that will help him or her develop into a lifelong learner with the critical thinking skills that are so sought after in the job market of our global economy?

The study of music is also a great self-confidence builder! Building confidence in children is crucial because it inspires them to put forth the effort necessary for real success. They believe in their own ability to succeed, so when they hit that inevitable bump in the road, they try even harder instead of giving up. This effort leads to real learning and development. This development becomes the foundation for increased confidence in the next round of effort.

Think of this as a process whereby success increases confidence, and effort leads to even more success, and so on. It's the cycle of success that we all want for our kids, isn't it?

Last but not least, learning to play the piano is downright fun! It's like having your cake and eating it too. Your child learns to do something that is incredibly joyous and fun, and all this other great educational stuff comes along with it by default. How can you go wrong?

How does *Play Piano in a Flash . . . for Kids* work? It works by eliminating what we have found are the two main barriers encountered in learning to play a musical instrument. These two barriers are:

1. Learning to read musical notation
2. The choice of songs used in many instructional methods for piano.

Play Piano in a Flash . . . for Kids will teach your school-age child to play nonclassical popular-style piano.

Of course, the time needed to learn to play and the amount of help possibly needed from an adult will vary according to the age of the child.

We want to be clear on this point: This book was designed to be read with or by the child. (Of course, this excludes the preface.) **It is not meant as a teacher's guide or "method book" per se.** Rather, it is meant to give a child the basic information necessary to launch him or her into a lifetime of wonderfully fun-filled, self-directed musical exploration.

The amount of assistance the child reading this book will need from you or someone else depends on their reading ability, age, and previous experience (if any) at a piano or keyboard.

No matter what the situation, we suggest you try to give the child the least assistance needed to get them started "down the hill." Your own judgment will be needed to figure out what that amount is. Please try, however, to break yourself from the locked-in paradigm you probably have of

learning to play piano = weekly traditional lessons

It's not that there is anything wrong with weekly lessons . . . far from it. In fact, we can't think of any reason that a child would not be very well served taking lessons given by a private teacher who embraces our chord style approach.

However, it is vital that a private teacher attempting to teach a child using this book acknowledge what we feel is a *crucial* distinction. That being the inherent difference between teaching classical-style piano and what we are doing in this book.

The weekly lesson regimen we're all familiar with which uses a traditional piano method's sequence of Book 1, Book 2, Book 3, etc., is the best way to go down the path of learning to become a good *classical* piano player, which is not where we are heading with this book and this style of instruction.

In fact, we believe that this style (the child's self-exploration of music that he or she enjoys, assisted when needed by you or a teacher) will provide a much richer and more meaningful path toward playing piano than some imposed, formal regimen.

No previous musical background is required by the child, or by the adult possibly assisting the child.

If you use the techniques shown in *Play Piano in a Flash . . . for Kids,* the obstacle of note reading is minimized because you only have to read a single note melody for the right hand and chord symbols for the left hand.

If this sounds like a foreign language to you already, don't despair. It is all very clearly explained in this book.

The type of musical notation we teach is called *lead sheet notation* and is used by most professional musicians around the world who play nonclassical music.

The second obstacle—choice of songs—is completely eliminated, because in *Play Piano in a Flash . . . for Kids* you learn to play piano by actually "playing" your all-time favorite songs.

This book is designed to quickly and efficiently share the essential information in each chapter; then, more in-depth enrichment information is given for most chapters in the Nuts & Bolts sections, found in the back of the book.

If an adult wants to participate in the learning process, these Nuts & Bolts sections are where your guidance would be helpful by discussing the concepts described with the child.

Will *Play Piano in a Flash . . . for Kids* teach your school-age child how to be a classical pianist? The answer is an emphatic *no!*

If you want your child to be able to play Bach, Beethoven, and Mozart, you should choose the route of traditional weekly piano lessons.

But if, on the other hand, you want your child to learn all of the other nonclassical styles of piano playing, as well as learn to play the piano for fun and recreation, *Play Piano in a Flash . . . for Kids* is the book for you.

Let's get started right now! Go ahead!

Read Chapter 1 with your future piano player. Reading Chapter 1 together will give you some insight as to how much adult help, if any, your child will possibly need during the process of learning to play piano in a flash.

Then get ready to share the joy of music.

The benefits will last a lifetime!

CHAPTER 1
INTRODUCTION

What kind of music do you like?

What are your favorite songs to listen to
   on the radio?

What kinds of CDs do you like to buy?

Every kid that I know has some pretty strong
opinions about music, so I'm sure that you didn't
have any trouble answering those questions.

But here is a question that might be a little
harder for you to answer: Have you ever watched
or heard someone playing one of your favorite
songs on the piano or keyboard and wished that
you were the one playing?

And then have you ever said to yourself, "Boy, I
sure would like to be able to play the piano, just
for fun! But I don't want to take piano lessons
every week and really practice a lot."

Maybe you have even tried to play the piano
before but it was just too hard, or you never
even got to play any of the songs you wanted to
learn how to play. You thought, "Oh well, forget
it. It's too hard!"

No, no, no!! Please, please don't forget it!! I have great news for you!

This book, *Play Piano in a Flash . . . for Kids,* has been written for kids just like you—kids who want to learn how to play what is called *popular-style piano* or, as you may think of it, playing piano "just for fun."

This book will teach you how to play piano the way you hear professionals play when you listen to CDs of music that you love.

At the end of the book, there is an extra section called Nuts and Bolts. Here you will find some extra information that you don't really need to actually start playing the piano—just some other stuff about music that you might like to know for fun.

Here's how it works!

While you are reading this book, either by yourself or with an adult, you will learn to play the piano in your own home. Whether you are taking weekly piano lessons or not.

Since you will be able to choose the songs that you want to learn how to play, you'll be able to learn as many or as few songs as you wish; in other words, you can learn at your own speed!

Now you might be thinking, "OK, this sounds pretty cool, but playing the piano still looks hard. How will I know which keys to push down? I don't know if I can play with both of my hands together. And I don't know anything about reading music notes."

Don't worry!

There are really only three things that you need to know:

1. Which key is which
2. Which key the music notes tell you to push down
3. How long to hold the keys down

After you learn those three things, playing the piano is just as easy as pressing a button to turn on a television or turning a light switch on and off! All you have to do is press a button, flip a switch, or push down a piano key. Anyone can do it, right?

Here's how we will learn the three things that you need to know to play the piano:

In order to know which key is which, you will need to learn that each key on the piano has a letter name. Remembering these letter names is not very hard, though, because for music note reading and keyboard letters, we use only the first seven letters of the alphabet (A, B, C, D, E, F, and G) for the white keys. Each time we get to the letter G, we simply start over again at A.

I'm sure that you can guess that this group of letters is repeated many times on the piano keyboard, since there are obviously more than seven keys! For now we're just going to be paying attention to the white keys. We'll learn the black keys a little later . . .

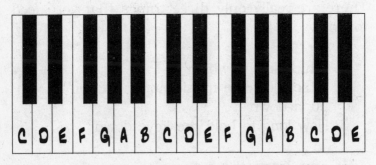

Names of White Notes Keep Repeating A Through G

Next, you will need to learn a little about reading music notes so that you will know which key on the piano to push and how long to hold it down.

Don't worry, though, because you will need to learn to read only one line of music notes at a time, not the several notes at a time that are found in regular piano sheet music.

It's kind of like when you were first learning how to read, remember? First you learned your letters. Then you learned how to read small words. Next you put the words together in a sentence. Now reading is easy, right?

Your right hand will be learning how to do pretty much the same thing. First, you will learn to read and play short combinations of notes (called a melody instead of a word), then longer and longer ones. After that, all you have left to learn is the four different types of notes and how long they last. You'll be able to play the melody of your favorite song in less than a week!

Learning how to play popular-style piano with your left hand is even easier because your left hand will not have to play as many notes as your right hand. It will be playing groups of notes called chords.

A chord is just more than one key pressed down at the same time. In our style of playing, most chords are either three or four notes played at the same time.

Also, most songs use only four or five chords, and many of the most common chords are used over and over again in lots of different songs.

Whenever you get ready to learn a new song, all you need to do is look at the chord charts in the back of this book to see what notes are in the chords found in that particular song.

Before long, you will know most of the common chords, and you will only have to look up any new chords that you might find in new songs.

That's it! That's all you have to know in order to play popular-style piano!

As you can see, it's a lot easier than learning how to play traditional classical-style piano and a lot faster too!

It's not that one style is better than another. They are just different.

Let's compare popular-style piano playing and classical-style piano playing to two sports. How about basketball and baseball?

One sport is not better than the other one. They are just different. Some people like one and some people like the other. Lots of people learn how to play both sports.

It's the same with piano playing. Some people like classical-style piano playing and some people like popular-style piano playing. And just like with sports, lots of people learn how to play both styles of piano playing.

Speaking of learning, let's get started!

Can you really learn how to play the piano?

Yes, you can!

You'll be playing your favorite song on the piano before you know it!

CHAPTER 2
WHICH KEY IS WHICH?

(Learning the Letter Names of the Piano Keyboard)

The piano is one of the simplest instruments in the world to play. It is just a matter of pushing buttons that are called keys.

It doesn't really matter if you've been playing the piano for one week or one year. If you push down a certain key, it will always sound the same. All you have to learn is which key to push and how long to hold it down.

It's as easy as playing a video game. Do you know how to use a video game controller? Can you remember which button controls which action in the game? Maybe not the very first time you played the game, but after a few games you didn't even need to think about it. Your hands just knew what to do. It's exactly the same with piano playing.

The first thing that you need to learn is which button or key controls which sound. So, which key is which?

Let's get started by learning our way around a piano keyboard.

Most keyboards have white keys and black keys. The black keys are placed in groups of twos and threes. We will call the groups of two black keys the twins and the groups of three black keys the triplets.

Try pressing down each black key twin on your piano and then each black key triplet. Remember, twins are groups of two black keys and triplets are groups of three black keys.

Now, let's find the lowest twin and the highest twin on your piano. Play a few twins and listen carefully. You will soon find by playing and listening that the lowest black key twin is on the left side of your keyboard and the highest twin is on the right side of your keyboard.

You can remember which side is which by remembering that the low sounds are on the left side because the words *low* and *left* both begin with the letter L.

It's the same for the black key triplets—the lowest triplet is on the left side of your keyboard and the highest triplet is on the right side of your keyboard.

By the way, if someone asks you to play "down the keyboard," it means play to the left. "Up the keyboard" means play to the right.

As we mentioned in Chapter 1, every key on the keyboard has a letter name. Let's learn the names of the white keys first.

The white keys of the keyboard use only the first seven letters of the alphabet, which are A, B, C, D, E, F, and G.

Each time you get to letter G, all you have to do is start over again with the letter A and keep going up in the same order.

You can see by looking at how many keys there are on your keyboard that each letter name will be used several times. No matter how many keys there are on your keyboard, the letters A, B, C, D, E, F, and G will simply be repeated over and over again.

You can sing this song to the tune of "The Alphabet Song" to help you remember not to go past the letter G when naming keyboard keys:

> A, B, C, D, E, F, G,
> There are seven letters you will see.
> Letter G is at the end,
> Start all over with A again.
> A, B, C, D, E, F, G,
> There are seven letters you will see.

Different sizes of keyboards have different numbers of keys. A full-size piano has 88 keys, but electronic keyboards may have less.

The size of your keyboard determines what the letter name of the first key on the left or right side will be. So the best way to begin finding your place on any keyboard is to find a special key that every keyboard has called *Middle C.*

Remember we said that the seven letter names are used several times on any keyboard? To find any C key, you need to find the key just to the left side of any black key twin.

An 88-key piano has eight C keys. How many letter Cs does your keyboard have?

Find each one and play it. Now, the Middle C we are looking for is—you guessed it—the C key that is closest to the middle of your keyboard. That's right—whatever C is closest to the center of your keyboard or piano is Middle C. Pretty simple, huh?

As soon as you know where all of the letter C keys are, it's as easy as A-B-C to find the other white key letter names because they actually are in A-B-C order, just like the alphabet.

The letters go from left to right on your keyboard, just like they do if you write them down or say them. See if you can name all of the white key letters as you push down each white key on your keyboard. With just a little practice, you will be able to name them quickly!

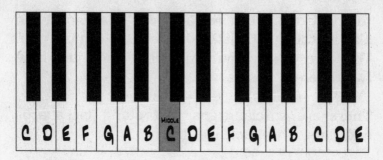

Middle C Is the C Closest to the Middle of Your Keyboard

Next, let's learn the names of the black keys. The black keys get their names depending on which white keys are on either side of them. This means that each black key actually has two names. These names are called sharp names and flat names. If you start on any white key and go to the black key on its right side, the black key will have a sharp name, such as F sharp. If you start on a white key and go to the black key on its left side, the black key will have a flat name, such as E flat.

Here is an example. Let's start on any D key. The black key to the right of the white key D is called D sharp and the black key to the left of the white key D is called D flat. This pattern works to name each black key. Choose another white key and see if you can name the black key on each side of it.

Notice that all of the black keys have two different names, depending on which white key you are using to name it. For example, the black key to the right of a C can be called a C sharp, or it can also be called a D flat. Don't let that confuse you. They are exactly the same note, they just have two different names.

There are special signs that stand for sharps and flats. They look like this:

sharp sign = ♯   flat sign = ♭

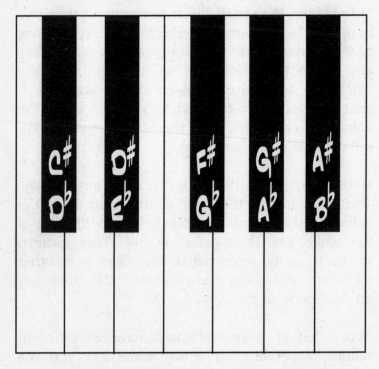

Black Keys Have Two Names—A Sharp Name and a Flat Name

Now we are ready to put the white keys and the black keys together! No matter how many keys you have on your keyboard, keyboards always have a basic group of 12 black and white keys that repeat over and over again. Notice that if you start on any key and start counting up letter by letter without skipping any keys, you can only count to 12 before you start repeating notes in the next set up the keyboard. Each set of any twelve notes is called an octave. Here is what they look like:

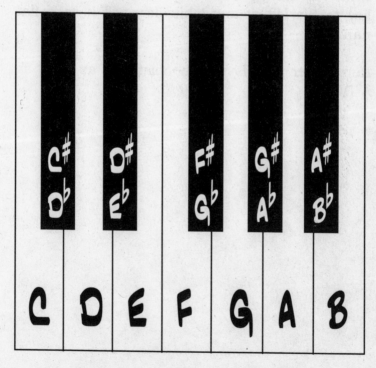

Here Are the Names of Every Key in One Octave

Try pushing down a few keys and see if you can name their letters. Remember that you can always find the correct letter name by starting on any letter C key (on the left side of any black key twin). Then, simply go through the musical alphabet (A–G) to find the right letter name.

Now that you know how to figure out what the keys are, you will never be lost! In just a few minutes, you will be able to name all of the white keys. Work on the black key names next. Don't forget that the black key to the right of any white key will have a sharp name and the black key to the left of any white key will have a flat name.

Remember . . . playing the piano is as easy as A-B-C!

CHAPTER 3
THE KEY TO READING MUSIC

(How to Read Music Notes in One Easy Lesson)

Now that you know the letter names of the keyboard keys, you are probably starting to wonder, "How will I know which key I am supposed to push down when I am playing a song? And how long am I supposed to hold each key down?"

In order to know which key to play, the next thing that we need to learn about is the connection between keyboard letter names, which we just learned, and the letter names of written music notes. If you have already learned how to play another instrument, maybe in your school band or orchestra, or if you have sung in your church or school choir, you may already know how to read written music notes. If that is the case, feel free to skim quickly through this chapter or skip it completely. For everyone else, let's get started!

In written music, the position of notes placed on the music staff tells us what to sing or play on any instrument. When we are playing the piano, the music notes tell us which key to push and how long to hold it down.

Whenever you look at a page of traditional piano sheet music, you will see two groups of lines hooked together on the left side with music notes written on them. There will be five lines in each group. Each group of these lines is called a music *staff*.

A music staff always has five lines, and in between the lines, four spaces. The lines and spaces are numbered from the bottom to the top of the staff. This means that the bottom line is line #1, the bottom space is space #1, and so forth.

At the beginning of each music staff, there will be a sign called a *clef* sign. Although there are others, the two clef signs used in traditional piano music are the treble clef sign, which is found at the beginning of the top music staff, and the bass clef sign, which is found at the beginning of the bottom music staff.

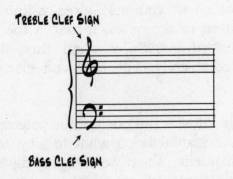

TREBLE CLEF SIGN

BASS CLEF SIGN

In traditional classical-style piano, music notes written on the treble clef staff (the top one) are played by the right hand and music notes written on the bass clef staff (the bottom one) are played by the left hand.

Since we are learning popular-style piano playing rather than classical-style piano playing, we will only be learning about and using the treble clef staff for our right hand to play the melody of a song.

Our left hand will be playing something called chords, which are not written on the bass clef staff. We will be learning in the next chapter that chord symbols tell us which chord to play and are simply written above the music notes on the treble clef staff.

So the good news is that we'll not need to worry about reading notes in the bass clef at all! Yippee!

Here is what you will need to know about music notes written on the treble clef staff:

Each of the five lines and four spaces on a music staff stands for a different key on the piano.

Do you remember that the piano keys have letter names from A to G? The lines and spaces of the staff also have these same letter names.

The letter names of the five lines, from bottom to top, are E, G, B, D, and F. Many people remember these letters by remembering this goofy saying:

Every Good Boy Does Fine

The first letter of each word is the letter name of a music staff line starting from the bottom line on the staff and going to the top line of the staff. So, the lines on the treble clef represent the notes (from the bottom to the top): E,G,B,D,F.

The letter names of the four spaces, from bottom to top, are F, A, C, and E. So an easy way to remember the spaces is to spell the word FACE.

If you go up the treble clef from the bottom line to the top line, and name each line and space, the letters are actually in A-B-C order, starting on line #1, letter E. The line and space letter names of the treble clef staff, beginning on Line #1, are E, F, G, A, B, C, D, E, F.

If there are any lines or spaces above or below the five lines of the music staff, you simply keep counting in A-B-C order (line, space, line, space) up or down from the staff until you get to the letter name of that particular line or space. These add-on lines (like you will find on Middle C) are called ledger lines.

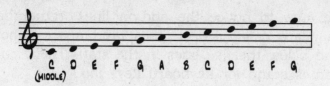

Line and Space Letter Names for the Treble Clef

Now that you can figure out the letter name of a note on the treble clef, don't forget that each line or space stands for a different key on the piano. The trick to reading piano music is to figure out which line or space in the music matches which key on the keyboard.

Guess what? If you go up the treble clef, from bottom to top in order, you will also find that the line and space letters name the keys on your keyboard, from left to right, and go up in order too!

We learned that the first line on the treble clef staff is letter E. But which E key is it on the keyboard? All keyboards have more than one letter E (and more than one of each of the other letter names, too).

The E note on line #1 of the music staff is the E key to the right of the Middle C key. From the picture that follows, you can see how the printed notes on the lines and spaces follow the keys on the keyboard.

Be sure to notice the add-on lines (remember, they are called ledger lines) and spaces above and below the five lines in the staff. Their letter names stand for keyboard keys too.

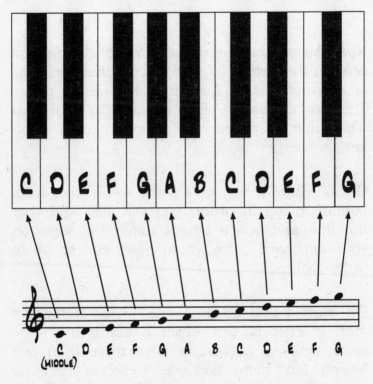

How Notes on the Treble Clef Staff Relate to the Keys on Your Keyboard

So now we know that the lines and spaces of the music staff have letter names that match the letter names of the keys on the keyboard. That still doesn't give us the answer to the question

"How will I know which key I am supposed to push down when I'm playing a song?"

Finally, here is the answer to that question!

In order to know which key to play, you will need to follow or read music notes on the treble clef staff.

Each music note's position on the lines and spaces of the music staff tells us the letter names of the keys to play and in what order to play them.

How does music note reading work? Here's how!

Music notes are made up of little circles that are called note *heads*. Sometimes they have sticks attached that are called note *stems*. (Note stems can point up or down, depending on the note's position on the music staff. They mean the same thing whether they go up or down.)

Notes are placed on either lines or spaces of the music staff. They are divided into sections called *measures*. The lines that divide the measures are called *bar lines*.

At the end of the last measure, you will see a double bar line to show that it is the end of the song.

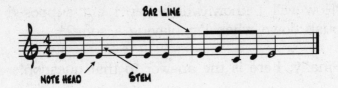

Remember that these lines and spaces of the music staff have letter names. Music notes are read from left to right, just like words in a book.

The line or space that the circle or note head of a music note is sitting on tells you its letter name and which key of the piano to play. Don't forget that if a note is sitting on a line or space above or below the five lines of the music staff, you simply keep counting stepwise (line, space, line, space) up or down the staff until you get to the letter of the note that you need to know.

A lot of kids use something fun called a *hand staff* to help them remember their staff letter names. Here's how it works!

Hold one hand in front of you with your thumb pointing down and your palm facing away from you. Your thumb and fingers are now the lines of the music staff (thumb is #1, pointer finger is #2, and so on). The spaces in between your thumb and fingers are the spaces of the music staff (space #1 is the space in between your thumb and pointer finger).

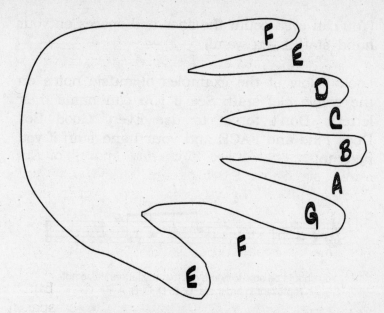

The Hand Staff Can Help You Remember Staff Letter Names

When you look at any note on the staff, the first thing that you have to decide is whether the note is a line note or a space note. Remember that you should check the position of the note head.

If the staff line is going through the center of the note head, the note is a line note. If the note head is sitting in a space (in between two lines), it is a space note.

As soon as you decide whether you are looking at a line note or a space note, then you will know which saying to use—Every Good Boy Does Fine for line notes or FACE for space notes.

(You can even count the lines and spaces on your hand staff if you want!)

Look below at the examples of music notes on the treble clef staff. See if you can name their letters. Don't forget to use Every Good Boy Does Fine and FACE and your hand staff if you need to.

You should be able to figure out that the letters these notes represent in order are: G, E, D, C, B, A, F#, G

"OK, now I know which key to push down," you might be thinking. "I know because I can figure out the letter names of music notes written on the treble clef staff, and they tell me which key to push down on the piano. But I still don't know how long I'm supposed to hold each key down!"

How long you hold onto a music note, or how long you hold a keyboard key down, depends on the type of music note that you are playing. Each type of note stands for a different amount of time. In music, time is measured by something called a beat, which is a lot like a second in real time. Here are the most commonly used types of music notes and their beat values:

o	Whole Note = 4 beats
♩ (half note)	Half Note = 2 beats
♩	Quarter Note = 1 beat
♪	Eighth Note = ½ beat (2 = 1 beat)

Eighth notes are usually connected like this:

If there is ever a dot after any of these notes (like the dotted half note), all you have to do is add half of the normal number of beats for that particular note to its usual beat value. For example, a dotted half note equals 3 beats because a half note usually gets 2 beats, and half of 2 is 1. If you add 2+1, the total is 3 beats. Any note can be followed by a dot. Usually dots are found after quarter notes or half notes, like this:

Whenever you see a music note, it stands for a sound. There are also signs in music that stand for silence. They are called rests.

Each note has a matching rest that stands for the same amount of beats as the note does. Anytime you see a rest mixed in with the notes of a melody, all you have to do is stop playing for the number of beats that the rest gets.

It is a good idea to keep your hands on the keyboard. If you take your hands off the keyboard and lay them down in your lap, you might not be able to find your place again fast enough!

Here are the most commonly used types of rests and their beat values:

	Whole Rest = 4 beats
	Half Rest = 2 beats
	Quarter Rest = 1 beat
	Eighth Rest = ½ beat

Try these easy rhythms by playing them on the E key just to the right of Middle C (the C closest to the middle of your keyboard, which is the key to the left of the twins) key of your piano. Remember to hold the key down for the number of beats that the type of note gets.

How did you do? It's not too hard, is it?

In popular-style piano playing, rhythms do not need to be played exactly as they are written. The notes are only guidelines for us to use when we are playing songs that we know. You should try to play the rhythms of songs that you know just like they would sound if you were listening to them or singing them.

If you find the rhythm part too hard to figure out using the rests, try just humming or singing the tune while you play and ignore the rests.

Do you know any songs that you can sing from memory? Of course you do! Did you learn them by reading music? Probably not . . .

Remember that music doesn't come from printed notes. Printed notes are just a way to record the music on paper to give you a guide to help you play a song that you haven't played before.

Always let your ears tell you whether something sounds good or not. It's for *you* to decide in this style of piano playing!

There you have it—everything you need to know about reading music in one easy lesson.

Now you know the answers to all of your questions:

- Which key is which?
- How do you know which key to push down?
- How long do you hold the key down?

Here is a review of the most important points:

1. Music notes written on a music staff tell us what to sing or play on any instrument. When we are playing the piano, the music notes tell us which keys to push and how long to hold them down.

2. Each of the five lines and four spaces on a music staff stands for a different key on the piano. For the nonclassical style of piano we are learning, we need to look only at the treble clef and we can ignore the bass clef.

3. Piano keys have letter names from A to G. The lines and spaces of the staff also have these same letter names.

4. The "key" to playing the piano is to figure out which music staff letter matches which key on the keyboard. If you go up the staff, from bottom to top, in A-B-C order, you will also find that the line and space letters name the keys on the keyboard, from left to right, in order too.

5. Each music note's position on the lines and spaces of the music staff tells us the letter names to play on our keyboard or piano and in what order to play them.

6. The line or space that the circle or note head of a music note is sitting on tells you its letter name and which key of the piano to play.

7. How long you hold onto a music note, or how long you hold a keyboard key down, depends on the type of music note that you are playing.

𝅝	Whole Note = 4 beats
𝅗𝅥	Half Note = 2 beats
♩	Quarter Note = 1 beat
♪	Eighth Note = ½ beat (2 = 1 beat)

It may seem like a lot to remember, but don't worry! In popular-style piano playing, when you are playing a song, you have to read only one note at a time.

That's all you have to do to play any melody or tune—just read the music notes, one note at a time, and play them in the order that they are written on the music staff.

It's just like reading words in a book out loud, except that this time, when you listen to the sounds that you are making, you will be playing real songs on the piano!

CHAPTER 4
WHAT DO I DO WITH MY RIGHT HAND?

(Learning to Play a Right-Hand Melody)

Now that you know how to read music, we need to learn what each hand is going to be playing. Let's start with your right hand.

Your right hand will be playing the melody (or what you think of as the tune) of any song that you learn to play.

What's a melody? A melody is simply single notes played or sung one after the other. When they are strung together, they make a tune or melody.

You may remember that earlier in this book, we said that learning how to play a melody is a lot like learning how to read. When you were learning how to read, first you learned your letters, then you learned how to read small words, and then you learned how to put words together in a sentence.

Your right hand will be learning how to do pretty much the same thing. First, you will learn to read and play short melodies with your right hand, then longer and longer ones. In no time, you'll be able to play the melody of your favorite song.

So let's try putting together what we have just learned about note reading in the last chapter with some real piano playing! Here is all you have to do:

Take a look at the familiar melody below, "Twinkle, Twinkle Little Star." You will see that almost all of the notes are on the lines and spaces of the treble clef staff. Only Middle C and D are under the staff. This is very common.

Most of the melodies that you will be playing will have notes that are between Middle C and the F that is the top line of the treble clef staff. (The reason is because these notes are easy to read and also easy to sing.)

Here is another look at the notes on the staff and which keys on your piano they represent.

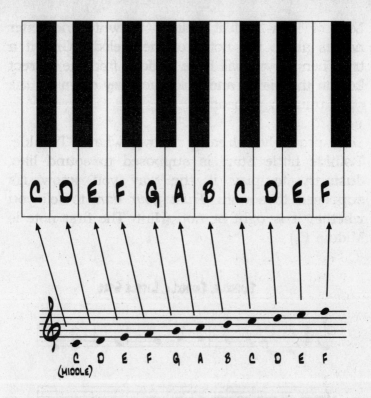

Now let's try to play a real melody! "Twinkle, Twinkle Little Star" begins on Middle C. Try playing the song with your right hand. Look at the chart above if you need to check where one of the piano keys is found.

Don't worry about which fingers to use on which keys. It's OK even if you only use one finger to start with! Right now, we are working on just playing the right keys by looking at the letter names of the notes on the music staff, and holding the keys down for the right amount of time. Remember, quarter notes (♩) get one beat and half notes (♪) get two beats.

Lots of kids find it helpful to write the letter names above the notes of the melody. Give it a try! Then all you will have to do is find the correct key on the piano, and hold each key down for the right number of beats.

You probably already know what "Twinkle, Twinkle Little Star" is supposed to sound like. Just try to play it the way you know it's supposed to sound. *Trust your ears* to tell you whether it is right or not. (Hint: The first note is Middle C.)

TWINKLE, TWINKLE, LITTLE STAR

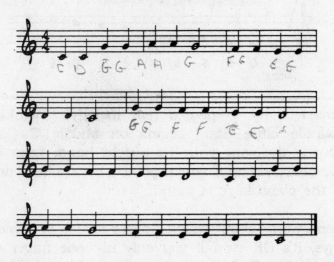

(Full-size copy available free at www.scotthouston.com/kidsbook)

How did you do? If playing this melody still seems a little hard to you, don't worry! After all, this is the first song that you have learned.

Each time you learn a new song, you will find that you remember more and more of the letter names of the keys and the notes on the music staff. Before you know it, you will not need to look at a keyboard chart or write in the letter names of the notes.

Let's try another song, called "Are You Sleeping?"

This song also starts on Middle C. It uses quarter notes, half notes, and a new note, the eighth note (♪).

In this song the eighth note stems are attached in sets of two (♫), but they are still just eighth notes. Since one eighth note gets ½ a beat, two attached eighth notes get one beat, so it uses the same amount of time as one quarter note.

Remember, it's OK to write your letter names above the notes for your right hand if that helps you play the song.

ARE YOU SLEEPING?

(Full-size copy available free at www.scotthouston.com/kidsbook)

Here are two more songs that you might already know. They both use the same types of notes (quarter note, half note, and eighth note) that you have already learned.

Go ahead! Write your letter names above the right-hand notes and try playing both of them.

By the way, at the end of this song, you will see two dots to the left of the double bar line. This is called a repeat sign. It just means to play the song again.

THIS OLD MAN

(Full-size copy available free at www.scotthouston.com/kidsbook)

In "Row, Row, Row Your Boat," you see some eighth notes hooked together in groups of four. They are played just the same (each note gets ½ a beat) whether they are by themselves, attached in twos, or attached in fours as they are here.

ROW, ROW, ROW YOUR BOAT

(Full-size copy available free at www.scotthouston.com/kidsbook)

For our last song in this chapter, let's try a song that you have probably heard at Christmas time, "Jingle Bells." You can see that this song uses the same types of notes as our other songs. The only different note is the whole note (𝑜) in the fourth and the eighth measure, which should be held for four beats.

JINGLE BELLS

(Full-size copy available free at www.scotthouston.com/kidsbook)

That's it! That's all you have to know to play the melody of any song on the piano with your right hand!

What should you do next?

Learn the melody to some more songs—that's what!

"What songs?" you ask.

"Aren't some songs too hard for me?"

The answer is no!

As long as you are going to be learning new melodies, you might as well be learning the melodies to songs that you like and you want to learn. Now all you have to do is get the printed music to that song . . . your *favorite* song.

By now you may be wondering where you can get printed music (or sheet music, as it is commonly called). A good place to start is at your local music store. You can find individual songs or collections of songs in books. You can also find music on the Internet for purchase. It may even be possible to borrow some music from your local library!

Now that you know how to get the sheet music, you know what to do next!

What are you waiting for?

CHAPTER 5
WHAT DO I DO WITH MY
LEFT HAND?

(Learning to Play Left-Hand Chords)

So far, we have learned

1. how to find the letter names of the piano keys,
2. how to read written music notes, and
3. how to play a melody with our right hand.

The next step is to learn what our left hand will be doing.

The left hand will *not* need to play notes that are written on the music staff the way that the right hand does. It will be playing things called chords.

What is a chord?

A chord is simply two or more notes played at the same time. Most of the chords that we will be playing will have either three or four notes.

The easy thing about chords is that your left hand needs to play just one chord for every chord symbol that you see up above the line of melody notes. Even better, there is usually only one chord symbol per measure.

Can you play more than one chord in each measure? Sure, it's up to you! But just to get started, let's learn some basic chord positions and try playing them one time in each measure of some of the songs that we learned in the last chapter.

You might be wondering how you will know which chord you are supposed to play. If you take a look at a page of written music, you will usually see some capital letters up above the melody notes in the treble clef staff.

Sometimes they have sharps, flats, numbers, or other letters after them. These are the *chord symbols*. They tell you which chord you should be playing with your left hand (while you are playing the notes that are written on the staff for the right hand).

What do these chord symbols mean? At first they might look like another language to you. However, they are really pretty simple to figure out because they all have only two different parts to figure out.

The capital letter at the beginning of the chord symbol (sometimes it is the only thing in the symbol) is the name of the *root* note of the chord.

When a chord is played in its basic (or root) position, the root note is the bottom (or lowest sounding, or farthest to the left) note of the three or four notes being played in the chord.

Just remember, the root note is at the bottom of a chord, like the roots are at the bottom of any plant. The other parts of the chord symbol are like the flowers and leaves on a plant. If you see only the root of a plant, you probably can't tell what kind of a plant it is, can you? The other parts of a chord symbol identify the different types of chords, just like flowers and leaves identify different types of plants.

In this book, most of the chords that we will learn are called *major* chords. The symbol for a major chord is a capital letter all by itself. If there is just a letter with nothing else after it, that tells you it is a major chord that should be played.

Look next at the music for one of the melodies that we learned in Chapter 4, "Are You Sleeping?" You will see some capital letter Cs up above the right-hand notes in the treble clef staff. These are the chord symbols.

Since the C is a capital letter all by itself without anything after it, it stands for a C major chord.

ARE YOU SLEEPING?

(Full-size copy available free at www.scotthouston.com/kidsbook)

Whenever you need to figure out how to play any chord, there are two things that you need to know:

1. What key should you start the chord on?

2. What shape is the chord . . . in other words, what other keys do you need to push down along with the root note?

Look at the following chart, which shows which keys your left hand needs to press down in order to play a C major chord. The shaded note on the chart is Middle C.

The chart shows us with the dots on the keys that the three keys in a C major chord are C, E, and G.

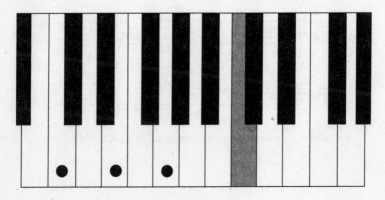

Notice that all three dots are to the left of the Middle C key (the shaded key). This is where most chords are played. You can expect most chord charts to show keys being played near the Middle C key or on the eight keys to the left of Middle C simply because chords sound better there.

Play a C chord near the bottom of the piano. How does it sound? Most people think it sounds very "muddy."

Now play a C chord where it is shown in the chord chart. See what we mean?

Chords just tend to sound nicer right around the middle of the piano, so that's where we tend to play them.

What key should we start on for a C major chord? Remember, the root note is the capital letter in the chord symbol, and it is the lowest note in the chord.

The starting (or lowest) note for a C chord should be played on the first C key to the left of the Middle C key. The next two notes in the C major chord are E and G. They should be played in between the root note C and Middle C. The chart shows you exactly which notes to play.

Try playing the C major chord a few times with your left hand. It's OK to use whatever fingers you want, but a good place to start is by using your little finger on the bottom root note, your middle finger on the E, and your thumb on the top G note. However, if that feels really difficult for you and something else feels more comfortable, go ahead and use whatever fingers you want to.

This is a great time to learn a little bit about the pedals. Take a quick peek under your piano or keyboard. You might see one, two, or three pedals that you can use with your feet. You are going to use only the *sustain* pedal (the pedal furthest on the right). You will want to press and hold it every time you play a chord with your left hand. It will allow you some time to locate your next chord by continuing to sound the chord even though you aren't still playing it. When you find the next chord, play it and then press down the sustain pedal again. Hold it until you play your next chord.

If your keyboard does not have a pedal, don't panic—you can purchase one separately from the manufacturer. The easiest way is to go your keyboard manufacturer's Web site.

Now, let's try playing with both hands!

While your right hand plays the melody of "Are You Sleeping?," your left hand should play a C major chord each time you see the chord symbol above the right-hand notes.

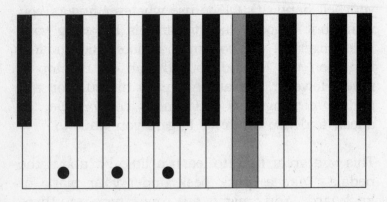

C

ARE YOU SLEEPING?

(Full-size copy available free at www.scotthouston.com/kidsbook)

How did you do? Don't worry if you are having trouble getting your hands to work together. After you have learned one or two more songs, it will get easier.

Playing two different things with your hands on the piano is a little like learning how to swim.

When you are swimming, your hands have to do one thing while your feet do something else. At first, it's hard to get them to work together, but, after a while, you don't even think about it, right?

It's the same playing with both hands at the same time on the piano. You have to do one thing with your right hand (play the melody) while your left hand does something else (plays chords).

Right now, it probably is a little difficult to get your hands to play together, but before long, you will barely have to think about it at all! Just focus on playing one measure at a time. Remember that a measure is the distance between two bar lines. So at the beginning of a new measure, start playing both hands at the same time.

Play the chord with your left hand and hold down the sustain pedal with your foot until you have played all the notes in the melody line with your right hand for that particular measure.

Then you are ready to play the next measure. So, again you will play the chord with your left hand. With your foot, you will press down the sustain pedal and hold it down until your right hand has played all the notes in the melody line for that measure.

Next, you guessed it: You will follow the same pattern for each measure until the entire tune has been played.

Here is another song that we learned in Chapter 4, "Row, Row, Row Your Boat." It also uses the C major chord.

See if you can play the chords with your left hand while you play the melody with your right hand.

Remember, you only have to play the chords one time for each time you see the chord symbol, then hold the sound using your sustain pedal with your foot. That's it!

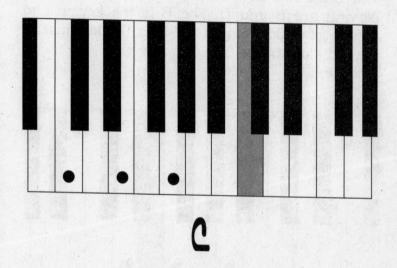

ROW, ROW, ROW YOUR BOAT

(Full-size copy available free at www.scotthouston.com/kidsbook)

Now, here's another chord, the G major chord.

What is the root note of the G major chord? G, of course!

If you look at the chart below, you will see that G is the lowest, or root note, of the chord. Play this note on the G to the left of the Middle C key.

The two other keys that your left hand will be playing are B and D. The B is the key just to the left of Middle C and the D is the key just to the right of Middle C.

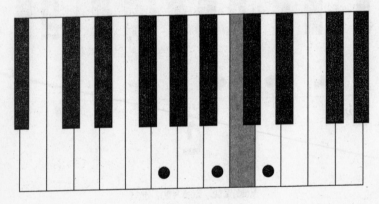

G

Try playing the G major chord a few times. Did you notice that your hand is in the same shape that it was in to play the C major chord?

You don't need to change the shape of your hand to play these two chords, you just need to change where you are placing your hand over the piano keys.

Imagine if you broke your left arm and the doctor put a cast on it that locked your hand in exactly the right position to play the C major chord. You would also be able to play a G major chord with that same cast on your hand.

The only difference would be whether your pinky was over the C key to play a C major chord or over the G key to play a G major chord.

Try switching your left hand back and forth from the C major chord to the G major chord a few times until you can make that jump easily.

Now you are ready to play "This Old Man," a song that uses the two chords that you have just practiced.

You'll find the charts of both the C and G chords, as well as the music to the song, on the next two pages.

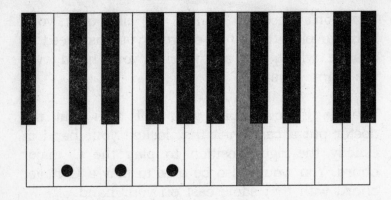

C

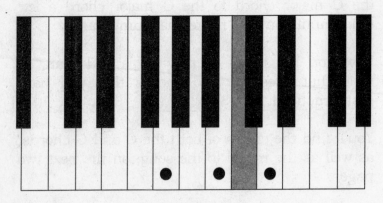

G

This Old Man

(Full-size copy available free at www.scotthouston.com/kidsbook)

For our third and final chord in this chapter, we will be learning the F major chord.

By now, you should know right away that the root note of this chord is F. As you can see in the chord chart, it should be played on the F key to the left of the Middle C key. The other two notes in this chord are A and C. The A should be played to the left of Middle C and the C should be played on the Middle C key.

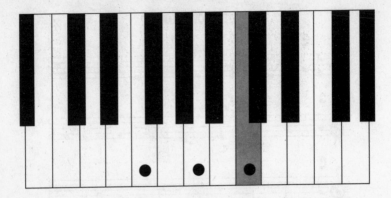

F

Try playing a few F major chords. Again, your hand is in the same shape (or the same cast!) as it was for the C major and G major chords. All three chords (C, F, and G) feel just the same to your hand; the only difference is what note you start them on, which is the root.

Before we play a song with the C major chord, the G major chord, and the F major chord, try moving your left hand between these three chords a few times. It will help if you remember to keep your hand in the same shape as you switch places on the keyboard. Just think about getting your pinky over the root of the chord and the other two fingers should kind of fall in place without much thinking on your part.

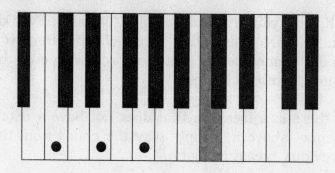

C

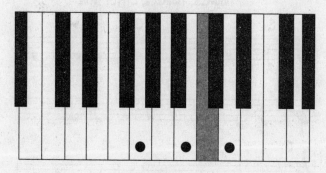

G

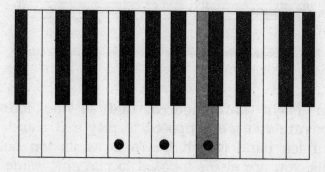

F

OK, now you are ready to play "Twinkle, Twinkle Little Star" using the three chords that you know. Remember to switch chords whenever the chord symbol changes.

If there is a measure that does not have a chord symbol above it, simply play the chord from the previous measure again.

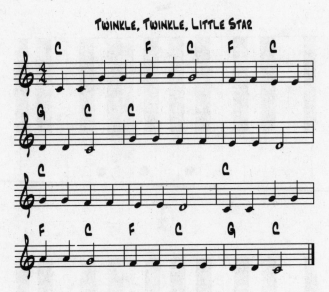

(Full-size copy available free at www.scotthouston.com/kidsbook)

You might have noticed that in the fourth measure you are supposed to play a G chord in your left hand (which has a D as its top note) while you are also supposed to play that same D as the melody note in your right hand.

Watch out—finger crash!!! Just kidding . . .

Actually, if that ever happens, it is no big deal at all. Just move your left-hand finger out of the way and get the melody note played with your right hand.

Earlier in this chapter, we compared a chord symbol to a plant, remember?

The capital letter of the chord symbol tells us the root or bottom note of the chord, just like the roots are at the bottom of a plant.

Any other parts of the chord symbol that come after the root tell us what kind of chord it is, just like the leaves and flowers on the plant that tell us what kind of plant it is.

Since we have learned only three major chords which don't have anything but the root in the chord symbol, we haven't seen anything else yet—but we will.

So how many kinds of chords are there?

Other than the major chords that we have been learning, the chart below shows you some of the most common kinds of chords that you might find in the songs that you want to play.

Of course, if you need to know how to play any of these chords, all you have to do is look at the position chart for that particular chord. Chord position charts for all of these chords are located in the back of this book.

Don't worry when you need to play chords that you don't know yet! None of these different types of chords are easier or harder than major chords—they are just different, that's all!

Chord Symbol	Root	Chord Type
C	C	Major
CMIN (or C-)	C	Minor
C7	C	Seventh
CMAJ7 (or CM7)	C	Major Seventh
CMIN7 (or C-7)	C	Minor Seventh
CAUG (or C+)	C	Augmented
CDIM (or C°)	C	Diminished

(Full-size copy available free at www.scotthouston.com/kidsbook)

There are a couple of other ways that you might see these chord symbols written. For example, sometimes a capital letter "M" is used to mean major and a lowercase m means minor. A dash, "—," is also sometimes used to mean minor. Also, every once in a while, you might see a plus sign, which stands for an augmented chord, and a small circle, which stands for a diminished chord.

As you learn more and more songs, you will also learn more and more chords and their symbols. It won't be long before you start remembering the chords that you play the most often, and then you won't always need to look them up on a chord chart.

Now it's time to think about your favorite song again. Have you learned how to play the melody yet?

What chords do you need to know so that you can play the song with both hands?

Your very favorite song is just waiting for you to play it. And now, you're ready!

CHAPTER 6
YIKES! HOW CAN I PLAY BOTH HANDS
AT THE SAME TIME?

(A Plan for Learning New Songs)

Now that you know how to play a melody with your right hand and some chords with your left hand, you are ready to start learning more and more songs.

Lots of kids find it helpful to have a plan of action to follow when tackling a new song. Here is a suggested plan:

1. Look at the chord symbols in your new song. Are there any chords that you don't already know? If so, check the chord charts and try playing them a few times.

2. Look at the right-hand notes on the treble clef staff. Write the letter names above the notes if you think that it will help you learn the song. (Pretty soon you probably won't need to do that, though, because you'll be getting so good at reading notes!)

This type of written music that we have been using for nonclassical music that has a melody line with chord symbols up above it is called *lead sheet notation*.

Lead sheet notation is most often found in special music books called *fake books*. That's a funny name, isn't it? A fake book!

Well, there is nothing fake about a fake book. It is just a nickname good musicians gave to big collections of lead sheets years ago. We will talk more about some different ways to use lead sheets and fake books in the next chapter.

The problem is that a lot of piano music is not written in lead sheet notation. Instead, it is written in the style of music notation that classical piano players use, because most piano players have never learned what you're learning in this book.

Most piano music looks similar to this:

"Oh, no!" you are probably thinking. "Where did all of these notes come from? I can't play this!"

Don't panic! You can play this because . . . guess what! You don't have to read all of those notes!

Here's how to take this kind of music apart and just read the parts that you need in order to play any song:

First, start at the top, up above the music staff. There you will see some letters. You know what these are! They are the chord symbols.

Below the chord symbols, in some music you might see some boxes with lines and dots in them. Those are guitar chord charts, so you can ignore them.

Next, look below the chord symbols and guitar chord charts. This is where you will see the regular music notation. There will be two music staffs—one with the treble clef at the beginning (it kind of looks like a fancy letter S) and one with the bass clef at the beginning (it looks like a backward letter C).

Remember, the treble clef staff is always the top staff, and it is the one that we read for our right-hand melodies. The bass clef staff has music notes for the left hand, but since our left hand will be playing the chords that the chord symbols tell us to play, *you can ignore the bass clef notes*.

That's it! On any sheet of written piano music, all you need to pay attention to are the chord symbols and the melody line notes in the treble clef!

If there is ever more than one note at a time in the treble clef notation, simply play the top note and ignore the others.

Whenever you are looking at a new song, just pretend that you are putting on special glasses that block out everything on the written music except the chord symbols and the treble clef notes, kind of like sunglasses that block out the harmful rays from the sun. It will change complicated music like this

into a lead sheet that you can read, that looks like this

Now, let's get back to our plan for learning new songs. Look below at the lead sheet for Beethoven's "Ode to Joy." What is the first thing that you are supposed to do when learning a new song? That's right! Check the chord symbols to see if you know all of the chords. In this song, you will need to know the C major chord and the G major chord. We have already learned both of these chords. Do you remember them? If not, check the chord charts below. Then try moving back and forth between both chords a few times.

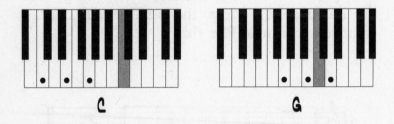

Next, look at the treble clef staff to check the notes in the right-hand melody. Go ahead and write the letter names above the notes if you need to. Then try playing the melody once or twice. Notice that at the end of the song, there are two sections labeled #1 and #2 with lines over them. The section labeled #1 has a repeat sign at the end of it. These are endings. All you have to do is play ending #1 the first time you play the song, and then play ending #2 the second time you play the song (do not play ending #1 again).

Now you are ready to play both hands together. Remember that your left hand has to play only one chord for each chord symbol found above the right-hand melody.

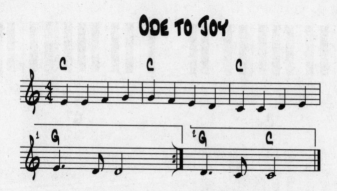

(Full-size copy available free at www.scotthouston.com/kidsbook)

Let's try another song!

How about "The Hokey Pokey"?

You know the plan for learning new songs . . .

First, check the chords. We already know the C major chord, but the G7 chord is a new one. Look at the chord charts below and practice playing both chords a few times. Because the G7 has four notes in it instead of three, you will need to figure out for yourself which fingers are most comfortable for you to use.

Next, write the letter names above the melody notes if you need to. Play the right hand alone once or twice, and then you're ready for both hands together.

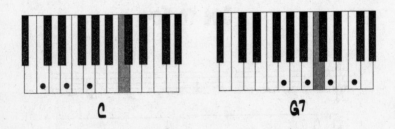

C   G7

HOKEY POKEY

(Full-size copy available free at www.scotthouston.com/kidsbook)

Here is another song that uses chords you already know—"When the Saints Go Marching In."

It uses the C major chord, the F major chord, and the G7 chord. Practice the chords. Write the letter names above the melody and give it a try.

WHEN THE SAINTS GO MARCHING IN

(Full-size copy available free at www.scotthouston.com/kidsbook)

Many songs can be written and played in different positions. Below is the same song that you just learned, "When the Saints Go Marching In," written in a different position.

Before you play it, look at the very beginning of the lead sheet notation. Right after the treble clef sign, you will see a flat sign. *(If you need to review what sharps and flats are, go back to Chapter 2 and take a look again.)*

Sometimes, music writers put flat or sharp signs at the beginning of songs, rather than beside each note that they want to be flatted or sharped. This particular flat is on line #3, which is letter B. It means that while you are playing the song, every time you come to a note that is a B you should automatically play a B flat instead of a B.

When you are writing the letter names of the melody above the notes, it would be a good idea to find all of the B notes and put a flat sign just to the left of them so that you will remember to play all of the B flats when you come to them in the music.

Next, check the chord charts and then you're ready to play "When the Saints Go Marching In" in this new position.

If you feel like your hand is having a hard time playing the C7 and B♭ major chords because your fingers can't reach the black keys, here's a little trick. Just push your hands an inch or two away from you and toward your keyboard so that the fingers that are on white keys can slide between the black notes on both sides of them. Good piano players don't always play white keys out on the very end. If they need to, they let their fingers slide up between the black notes on the keys to keep their hands comfortable and relaxed while playing chords.

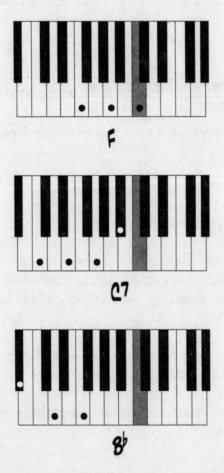

F

C7

B♭

WHEN THE SAINTS GO MARCHING IN

(Full-size copy available free at www.scotthouston.com/kidsbook)

How are you doing?

Now let's try playing a couple of songs written in regular piano music notation instead of what we have been reading, which is called lead sheet notation.

See if you can find the parts of the music that you need in order to play the songs.

Remember, you can ignore everything except for two things:

1. The chord symbols, and
2. The notes in the treble clef staff.

Then, follow our two-step plan for learning new songs:

1. Check the chords, and look up the charts for any new ones you might not know.
2. Then write the letters above the melody notes if you need to.

First, let's take a look at the regular piano music for "Jingle Bells." Check the chord symbols. You will need three chords to play this song: C major, G major, and D7.

We already know all of these chords except D7, which is a new one. Look at the chord charts below and practice switching from chord to chord with your left hand a few times.

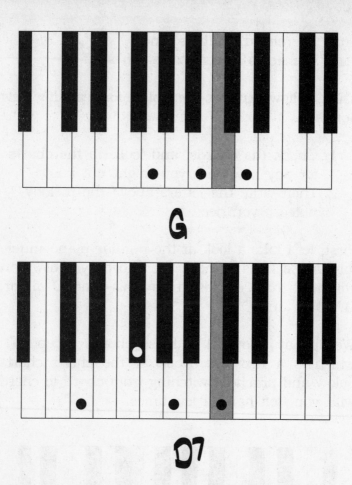

G

D7

Next, look at the treble clef melody notes. Remember, if there is ever more than one note stacked together, you will play only the top one. Write in any melody note letter names that you might need. Then try playing the melody.

If you have trouble finding the top note of the melody on the written music quickly enough while you are playing, use a marker to highlight the notes with a little dot right on the note head.

That way, when you are playing, you will quickly see the notes of the melody.

OK, now we're ready to play "Jingle Bells" with both hands. Don't forget—all you have to read are the melody notes and chord symbols. Ignore all other notes, rests, and musical signs.

JINGLE BELLS

(Full-size copy available free at www.scotthouston.com/kidsbook)

You sounded great, didn't you? Now you know that playing the piano isn't as hard as it looks!

You also now know that it's no problem when you want to learn a song that you can find printed only in regular piano music rather than lead sheet notation. You just ignore everything but the chord symbols and melody notes.

For our last song in this chapter, we are going to learn a song that everyone needs to know how to play—"Happy Birthday." Just think how pleased everyone will be when you can play "Happy Birthday" on the piano the next time one of your family or friends celebrates a birthday!

Like always, all you have to look at is the chord symbols and the melody notes. So, let's get started!

The chords in "Happy Birthday" are G major, C major, and D major. Check the positions on the chord charts below and practice them if you need to.

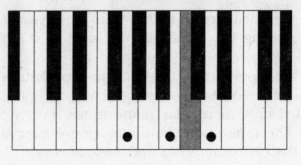

G

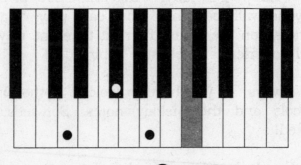

D

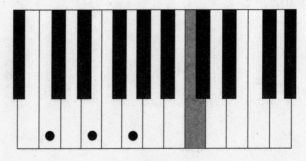

C

Look at the melody, and write the letter names above any notes that you might have trouble remembering. Don't forget to remember that any F in the melody line needs to be played as an F# because of the sharp symbol at the beginning of the song that is sitting on the F line. Try playing the right hand alone once or twice, and then you're ready to play the whole song.

HAPPY BIRTHDAY

(Full-size copy available free at www.scotthouston.com/kidsbook)

Nice job! Did you realize that you already know how to play nine songs? Is that cool or what? Now that you know the plan for learning new songs, nothing can stop you from learning more and more and more!

What about that favorite song of yours? Have you learned it yet? Why don't you play it right now, and make it song #10 in the growing list of songs that *you* can play on the piano!

Chapter 7
Playing from a Fake Book
Isn't Fake

(Learning More About Lead Sheet Notation)

The kind of written music that we have been learning to play is called *lead sheet notation*.

A song written in lead sheet notation is simply a "single note at a time" melody line in the treble clef with chord symbols up above it. Lead sheet notation is most often found in music books called *fake books*.

Why do they call them fake books? It is just a nickname professional musicians started using years ago and now everyone uses the term fake book to describe a big collection of lead sheets.

There is nothing fake about a fake book! A fake book is simply a music book that is full of lead sheets. Often, fake books are collections of a certain type of music such as pop/rock music, country music, or Christmas music.

Fake books are what professional piano players use when they are playing in public. Many people are surprised to learn that most professionals don't read regular piano sheet music. They read lead sheets, which are found in fake books.

Piano players like using lead sheets because they allow you to be more creative than reading regular piano sheet music. In lead sheet notation, the written notes are really only guidelines to the melody, the rhythm, and the chords.

When using a lead sheet, all you are required to do is to play a one-note melody with your right hand and play at least one chord per measure with your left hand. Other than that, you have the freedom to make your own music. Within the framework of the music written on the lead sheet, you can play a song pretty much however it sounds good to you.

You won't just be playing someone else's arrangement of a song! You will be playing what the songwriter actually wrote, and then creating (or *faking*—that's where they got the nickname) and playing your own arrangement!

As you read and play more lead sheets, you will become a great piano *player,* as opposed to a great piano music *reader.*

Now let's get some more practice in playing lead sheets.

Look below at the lead sheet notation and chord charts for the song "America."

Remember our plan for learning new songs? First, check the chord symbols to see if you know all of the chords in that particular song. If you don't know all of them, check the chord charts below.

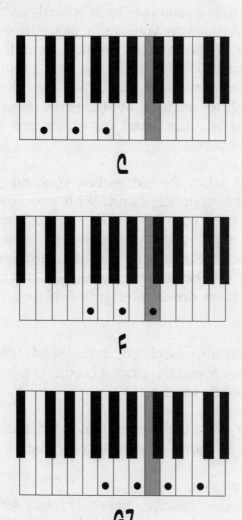

C

F

G7

Practice moving from chord to chord. Feel free to play as slowly as you need to make the chord jumps.

Now let's try to make that a little easier by holding the sound of each chord using your sustain pedal with your right foot. Once you get the hang of the sustain pedal, it actually makes your chord playing with the left hand easier. Why? Because once you "grab" the chord with the pedal to keep it sounding, it gives you a chance to lift your hand up earlier and move to the next chord.

To repeat what we did earlier, you will play the chord with your left hand. With your right foot, you will then press down the sustain pedal and hold it down until you play the next chord. When you are ready to play the next chord, lift your foot off the sustain pedal for a moment and press it back down after you've played the next chord.

So the pattern is chord, pedal (and hold down until you play the next chord), chord, pedal, chord, pedal, etc. . . .

After you can play the left-hand part fairly easily, it's time to move to playing only the right-hand part.

Look at the melody line of notes. Write any needed letter names above the notes in the right-hand melody.

Notice that we said any "needed" letter names. By now, you are probably starting to recognize some of the right-hand notes in the treble clef, and you might not need to write in all of the letter names anymore. Feel free to write in only the letter names that will help you. Pretty soon, you won't need to write in any letter names at all!

Is there anything else in the right-hand melody that might give you a problem? Do you need to write in any sharps or flats?

Feel free to play the melody through a couple of times if you need to. Now you are ready to put it all together—playing the song with both hands.

Just focus on playing one measure at a time. Remember that a measure is the distance between two bar lines.

At the beginning of a new measure, start playing both hands at the same time. With your left hand, play the chord and hold down the sustain pedal with your foot until you have played all the notes in the melody line with your right hand for that particular measure.

Then you are ready to play the next measure. So, again you will play the chord with your left hand. With your foot, you will press down the sustain pedal and hold it down until your right hand has played all the notes in the melody line for that measure.

Next, you guessed it: You will follow the same pattern for each measure until the entire tune has been played.

AMERICA

(Full-size copy available free at www.scotthouston.com/kidsbook)

How did you do? You're probably starting to get better at learning new songs, right? OK, let's try another one!

Next is the lead sheet for "She'll Be Comin' 'Round the Mountain When She Comes."

You know what to do! First, check the chords and look at their charts. Second, look at the melody and write in any letter names and sharps or flats that you might need as reminders.

It is almost always a good idea to practice playing the left- and right-hand parts separately before you try playing both hands together, but it's up to you. Sometimes you may know a song so well that you don't think it's necessary. Then you are ready to play it with both hands.

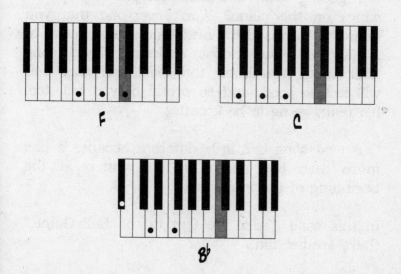

F

C

B♭

She'll Be Comin' 'Round the Mountain

(Full-size copy available free at www.scotthouston.com/kidsbook)

Is it getting easier and easier for you to play new songs on the piano? Won't everyone that you know be surprised the next time you are close to a piano and you sit down and start playing song after song? You know they will, and then you will feel so good, and so proud of yourself, too! It's really going to be great!

Our next song is a little different because it has more than one sharp or flat written at the beginning of the music staff.

In this song, "Take Me Out to the Ball Game," there are two flats.

Just like you did when there was only one flat, you just have to figure out which notes will have to be flatted by looking where the flat signs are placed and then write flat signs to the left of those notes in the melody so you will remember to flat them when you get there.

The flat signs are on line #3 (B) and space #4 (E), so those are the notes that you will be looking for when you are writing in the flats—B and E.

Don't forget to check the chords. You will notice right away that this song has more chord changes than we have been used to seeing. Don't let that worry you!

Again, you don't have to do anything different. Just check all of the chord positions on the chord charts. Then practice playing all of them and moving from chord to chord smoothly.

Also, if you come to any measures that don't have a chord symbol above it to tell you what chord to play, just repeat whatever chord was in the previous measure. Simple! Leave your left hand right where it was and play the same chord again.

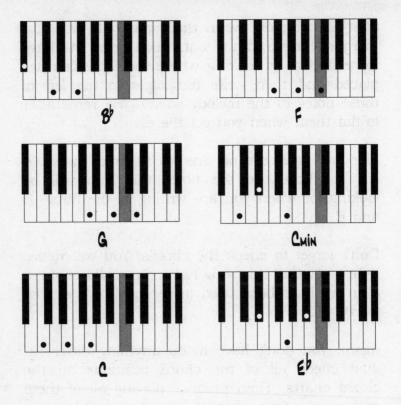

B♭

F

G

Cmin

C

E♭

After you can play the left-hand chords pretty easily, take a minute and play through the right hand alone.

As you play this song, you will notice a new symbol next to a note called a natural sign that looks like this:

natural sign = ♮

The job of the natural sign is to take away a sharp or flat on the note it is directly in front of—in other words, the natural sign tells you *not* to sharp or flat a note that you would have, and to instead just play the white "natural" key instead. In this song it occurs in the ninth measure, where in the melody you should play a G, then a G flat, then a regular old G (natural) again.

Take Me Out to the Ball Game

(Full-size copy available free at www.scotthouston.com/kidsbook)

Next we're going to talk about some creative ideas that you might want to try in your piano playing as you get more and more comfortable, and as you learn more and more new songs.

But, as you try these new approaches to playing for each hand, don't forget about our foolproof plan for starting new songs that we have been using over and over:

1. Check the chords and look up the charts for any new ones you might not know.

2. Play the left-hand chords alone and get comfortable moving from chord to chord.

3. Write any needed letters above the melody notes and play the melody line by itself a few times.

Chapter 8
Some Fun Tricks that Sound Great!

Here are some suggestions that will make your right-hand playing sound a little more creative and professional.

For every suggestion, there is an audio example of what we are talking about that you can hear for free from our Web site at this address: http://www.scottthepianoguy.com/kidsbook

Since music is so much more of a listening art than a written art, we really suggest you go to hear these examples as they are much easier to figure out and play correctly when you hear them in addition to reading about them.

[A] Raising the Melody Line One Octave

The first idea for your right hand is to play the melody line one octave higher than it is written.

You might remember that an octave is just an interval between notes. More specifically, an octave is the key that has the same letter name in the next set higher or lower from the one you are on.

For example, if you are playing a C and you count eight notes higher or lower, you will be on the next C one octave higher or lower.

If you want to play the melody one octave higher and the written melody begins on Middle C, all you have to do is begin playing on the next C key higher than Middle C, and then continue playing the melody in that higher position on the keyboard.

Try playing this melody an octave higher than it is written here:

KUM-BA-YAH

The chords in this song are: C major, F major, G7, and D minor.

We have played all of these chords before, except for the D minor chord. Check the chord charts below and try playing all of the chords. Practice moving between the C major chord and the D minor chord because you will need to play these two chords one right after the other in this song.

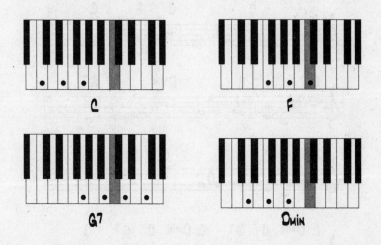

Now try playing the melody of the song. Feel free to play it a couple of times until you feel comfortable playing it.

You might want to play the song in the written position first, and then play it again with the melody an octave higher. See how you can hear the melody a little bit more clearly when it is played an octave higher on the keyboard. (That is the reason that sopranos, the highest voice heard in a choir, often sing the melody line.)

Remember to use your own ears as a guide. If you like it better played up an octave, go ahead and do it! It's your decision. If you like it better played in the same location that it is written, that's fine too. You be the judge . . .

KUM-BA-YAH

(Full-size copy available free at www.scotthouston.com/kidsbook)

B Playing the Melody Line in Octaves

Next, let's try another neat-sounding trick and play the whole melody of this song in octaves.

That means that you will play the written note and the note one octave higher at the same time. Wow! Two notes in your right hand at the same time! (Don't worry, it isn't as hard as it sounds.)

Look again at the melody for "Kum Ba Yah." The first note in the melody is Middle C. If you are going to play the melody in octaves, you should play Middle C and the C key to the right of Middle C at the same time.

Most people use their thumb on the lower note and their little finger on the higher note, but you can use whatever fingers are comfortable for you.

First, practice playing the entire right-hand melody in octaves, then add the left-hand chords and play the whole song that way. Sounds pretty good, huh?

C Filling in Chords with Your Right Hand

Another way to "spice up" the melody is for the right hand to play chords that match the left hand during empty spots in the tune. These should be played up higher on the keyboard than the melody. This is a little harder, because the right hand has to actually move out of its position to a higher position (the next octave higher), play a chord, and then move back into position.

The extra chords in the melody can be played together, like a chord usually is, or one note at a time. This technique works best when used with a slow melody that has some long notes (empty spots), such as "Amazing Grace."

"Amazing Grace" uses three chords we've used before: F major, C major, and B-flat major. Check the chord charts below and practice the chords once or twice. For this song, you should practice the chords with both the right and left hands, since you might be playing some of the chords in the right hand during the empty places in the melody.

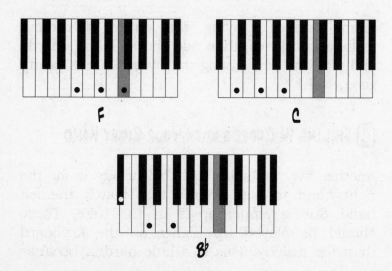

As always, you should then look at the melody and write in any letter names that you might need.

Try to find some places where there are some longer spaces between the notes in the melody. These are the places that you might want to have your right hand move higher, into the next octave up, and play a chord.

Here is the lead sheet for "Amazing Grace." Try it first as it is written. Then play it with some chords in the right hand to fill in some empty-sounding spaces.

(Full-size copy available free at www.scotthouston.com/kidsbook)

Remember that it is always OK to play the same chord that your left hand is playing anywhere else on the keyboard with your right hand, too.

Since they are the same notes, just played in different octaves, you can be assured that they will sound nice together. Just let your ear be the guide and feel free to experiment a little until you find something that sounds nice to you.

Now let's talk about some ideas for the left hand . . .

[O] PLAYING MULTIPLE CHORDS PER MEASURE

A very easy way to make your left hand playing sound a little more interesting is simply to play more than one chord per measure. All you have to do is repeat the left-hand chords in a steady rhythm.

So far, we have been playing only one chord at the beginning of each measure and holding it down or keeping it sounding with the pedal.

Now you are going to try playing the chords two or three or even four times per measure in the song "Oh Susannah."

Don't forget to watch the chord symbols so that you will remember to change chords at the right time. You shouldn't have any trouble because this song uses only three chords you probably know well by now: C major, G7, and F major.

Play the melody through one time to make sure that you know all of the letter names. Then you will be ready to play both hands together.

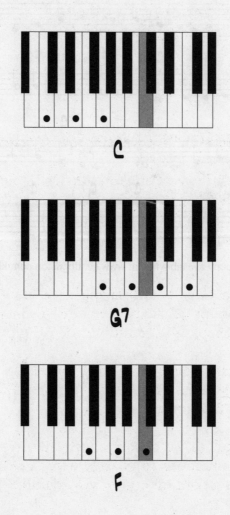

C

G7

F

Oh, Susannah

(Full-size copy available free at www.scotthouston.com/kidsbook)

Ⓔ Rhythmic Patterns with Chords

Another approach to playing repeated chords is to actually play a rhythm with your left hand as you are repeating the chords.

Again, don't forget to watch the chord symbols so that you will remember to change chords at the right time.

In the beginning, it probably is a good idea to decide what rhythm you will be using with your left hand so that you won't have any trouble keeping your hands together.

If you are having trouble getting your two hands to work together when you try to play rhythms with your left hand, just remember to slow way down to give your hands a chance to get used to the new rhythms they are learning to play.

In the next song, "He's Got the Whole World in His Hands," you only have to use the same two chords we used in "Oh, Susannah," the C major chord and the G7 chord. Practice playing a rhythm with these two chords, check the notes in the melody, and then try playing both hands together.

He's Got the Whole World in His Hands

(Full-size copy available free at www.scotthouston.com/kidsbook)

[F] Playing Only Roots with Your Left Hand

Playing only the root note of each chord is an unusual but interesting way of playing chords with your left hand. It is very easy to do—just play the lowest note of each chord rather than the entire chord. Even though it is a lot less notes, sometimes it can sound really nice to only be playing the root note of the chords and the melody. It is a very "open" sound.

Take a look at our next song, "Yankee Doodle." In this song, you will need to play the G major chord, the C major chord, and the D major chord. Their charts are below. Try playing the chords first as usual, but then try playing just the root notes and notice how different it sounds.

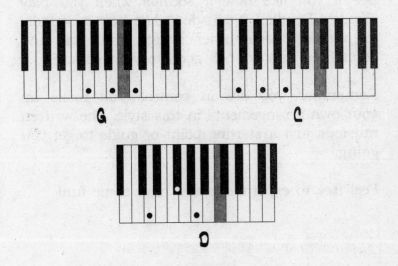

Of course, you know that your next step is to check the melody to see if there is anything that you need to mark or practice.

Notice that there is a sharp at the beginning of this song. It is on staff line #5, which is letter F. Don't forget that this means that you will have to sharp every F as you play the song. It's a good idea to write in a sharp sign to the left of every note that is an F before you play the song just to make it easier to remember.

A good suggestion for this song is to play it with the chords as written first, then play the melody with just the root note one time through, and then finish your arrangement by again playing the song with the chords as written.

See if you like how it sounds when you play "Yankee Doodle." If you don't like how it sounds, keep trying some other things until you find something that sounds good to your ears.

Remember, you are in control! You make up your own arrangements in this style. The written music is just a starting point or guide to get you going.

Feel free to experiment and have some fun!

YANKEE DOODLE

(Full-size copy available free at www.scotthouston.com/kidsbook)

Ⓖ Root First, Then Chord

One of the most popular ways of playing chords is to play the root note of the chord first and then the rest of the chord. Most of the time, this pattern is played one time in each measure.

For example, if you are playing the C major chord, you should play the root note C alone, and then play the two other notes, which are E and G together. Keep repeating this pattern until the chord symbol changes. Then play the same pattern on the next chord.

Try playing "Yankee Doodle" again. This time, play the root first, and then play the rest of the chord. When you get a little better at playing this pattern, it's OK to play the pattern two times in each measure.

Another variation of this one (although a little more difficult) is to play the root down one octave from where you normally play the chord. Then you come up to the normal position to play the chord. Although this takes a little more "target practice" because your left hand is jumping back and forth, it really sounds nice and is worth the effort.

(H) BROKEN CHORDS

Another approach to playing chords is to "break them up." This means to play each note of the chord separately. Playing broken chords is easy!

All you have to do is start on the lowest note and play upward, from the lowest note to the highest note, and then play downward, from the highest note to the lowest note.

Look at the chords in our next song, "Michael, Row the Boat Ashore." These three chords, C major, F major, and G major, are all familiar chords.

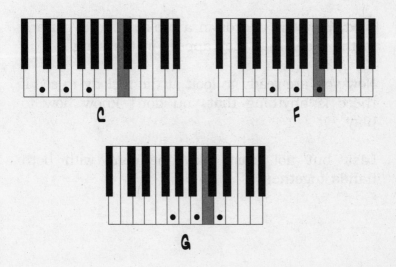

Try playing each chord in a "broken chord" pattern, as shown below:

C major C, E, G, E
F major F, A, C, A
G major G, B, D, B

For example, when you get to a C chord in a measure, rather than play all three notes at the same time, play just the C on the first beat, then just the E on the second beat, then just the G on the third beat, then back down to just the E again on the fourth beat.

Notice that your hand position can stay the same whether you are playing the full chord or breaking up the chord into individual notes.

Next, play the chords in a broken chord pattern in the order that they appear in the song.

Now you are ready to look at the melody to see if there is anything that you don't know how to play.

Last, but not least, play the song with both hands together.

MICHAEL, ROW THE BOAT ASHORE

(Full-size copy available free at www.scotthouston.com/kidsbook)

How did you do with all of these different ways of playing melodies and chords?

Isn't it great how you can play a song in all of these different ways even though the music stayed the same?

The ideas described here are just a few of the many ways to change the melodies and chords of all of the songs that you play. There is no limit to the possibilities!

That is why playing from lead sheets is such a great way to play nonclassical music. It lets *you* decide how you want to play a song, and lets you play whatever way your ear likes it best. It's all up to you!

Don't be afraid to try any and all of your own ideas. If it sounds good to you, then it is good!

Remember, there is no right or wrong way to play your songs on the piano. It's time to just start playing the piano and having some fun! It's time to make your own kind of music!

CHAPTER 9
ACCOMPANIMENT-STYLE PLAYING
OR
HOW TO PLAY ALONG WITH OTHER PEOPLE

Now that your piano playing is getting better and better, other people may begin asking you to *accompany* them while they sing or play another instrument.

What is accompaniment or accompaniment-style playing?

It means that you will play some background music on the piano while the other person is singing or playing another instrument. You have probably seen other people playing the piano this way many times.

"But that looks hard," you may be thinking. "I'm not that good yet. My piano playing might mess up the other person's playing or singing."

Well, here's the good news: Accompanying is not as hard as it looks or sounds! And now that you know how to play some chords, you can learn how to accompany your friends or family or anyone else who might ask you.

Did you know that many students earn a little extra money by accompanying other kids when they perform at school, in church, or in contests? Others just get together with their friends and play music for fun!

Here's all you have to do!

The easiest way to accompany another person is to play the chords of the song with your right hand while playing the root note (whatever the letter name is in the chord symbol) with your left hand.

What about playing the melody with the right hand like you have been learning to do in the earlier chapters of this book?

In accompaniment-style playing, you don't have to worry about playing the melody at all! The person that you are accompanying will be playing or singing the melody while you play the accompaniment on the piano.

What? Just play chords? Don't play the melody? Sounds easy, right?

You're right! You might even find that accompaniment-style playing is easier than the pop-style playing that you have been learning.

Let's give it a try!

You can practice accompaniment-style playing on any one of the songs that we have already learned. How about "Happy Birthday"? There will always be plenty of occasions when someone will want to sing "Happy Birthday," and now you will be able to play the accompaniment on the piano.

Here is the lead sheet for "Happy Birthday":

Remember that in accompaniment-style playing, all you have to look at is the chord symbols that are found above the melody notes. The only difference in this style is that you will be playing the chords with your right hand, rather than with your left hand.

First, try making the chord changes in "Happy Birthday" with just your right hand. Then you should practice playing the root note of each chord with your left hand. Next, you are ready to try playing with your hands together to see how it sounds. What do you think? It sounds pretty weird, huh?

You're probably thinking that this style of playing doesn't sound as good as solo-style piano playing like we have been doing so far in this book. But you know why, don't you?

Of course, that's right! It's because neither one of your hands is playing the melody. If you want to hear how the song is really supposed to sound, you will need to hum or sing the melody as you play.

Try it! Hum or sing "Happy Birthday" while you play the chords with your right hand and the root notes of each chord with your left hand.

Pretty cool, huh? Now the song sounds the way it's supposed to sound! You might be wondering if using this method of accompaniment-style playing will work with any song written on a lead sheet. It sure will!

So whenever other people start asking you to accompany them while they sing or play any instrument, don't hesitate. Now, accompaniment-style piano playing is something that you know how to do!

Chapter 10
Now You're Starting to
Play Like a Pro!

Can you believe it? You *can* play the piano!! And not just the tunes in this book, but much more importantly the songs that you love to listen to on your audio CDs, and your favorite songs that you hear on the radio and in the movies.

Wasn't it a nice surprise to learn that it's the same kind of piano playing that many professional musicians do? And now, you know how to play the piano too!

This book has taught you the skills to learn any new popular-style song that you want to learn. What are those skills? They are:

1. You need to be able to identify the letter names of the notes in the treble clef.
2. You need to know how to build chords or have chord charts available.
3. You need to memorize the few chords that are in the song that you want to play.
4. You need to play the melody line with your right hand and the chords with your left hand.

That's not so hard, is it? Of course not! Think about how many songs you have already learned, just by reading this book and playing the songs in it.

Is there a lot more to learn? Sure, there is always more to learn about any topic, and we hope that now you can have some fun playing songs right away, you will want to continue to learn more and more.

But do you need to know everything about piano playing just to get started and learn how to play some songs for fun? The answer is *no*!

How far can you go?
As far as you want!

How many songs can you learn?
As many as you want!

What about that favorite song of yours that we have been talking about?
Have you learned it yet?

Now you know everything that you need to know to get started on your favorite song or any other song that you want to learn.

What are you waiting for?

Go have fun playing, not practicing, the PIANO!

Appendix A
List of Songs Included in the Book

Appendix B
"Nuts & Bolts" Follow-Up Info for Chapter 2

In music, there is a special way to measure the distance between notes or sounds. Rather than using inches or feet, we use something called intervals.

The smallest interval is called a half step. The easiest way to learn about half steps is by looking at a keyboard. One half step is the *closest distance between two keys* with no other keys in between them. For example, from the C key to the C sharp key is one half step.

Because of the layout of a keyboard, half steps on a keyboard are usually between a white key and a black key, although there are two exceptions, which are between the B and C keys and between the E and F keys.

Those are the two places on a keyboard where there is no black key between the white keys.

Because the rule is *closest distance between two keys,* those distances are only half steps.

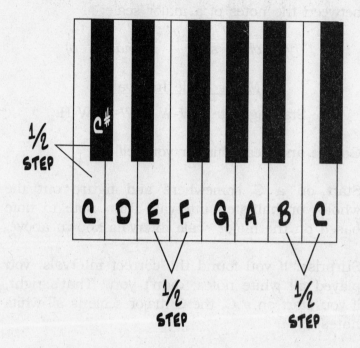

Not surprisingly, two half steps make a whole step. On the keyboard, a whole step is the distance between any two keys with one key in between them, such as from C to D.

By knowing how to find half steps and whole steps from one note to another, you can very easily figure out something called a *scale.*

A scale is just a bunch of notes separated by a particular order of whole- or half-step intervals.

Although there are many different types of scales, the most important one is called a major scale. Here are the whole and half step intervals between the notes of a major scale:

(W= whole step   H= half step)

<u>Major Scale Intervals</u>

Starting note - W-W-H-W-W-W-H

Go see and hear this for yourself!

Start on a C somewhere and figure out the whole- or half-step intervals from note to note based on the major scale intervals shown above.

Surprise! If you found the correct intervals, you played all white notes, didn't you? That's right, if you start on a C, the C major scale is all white notes!

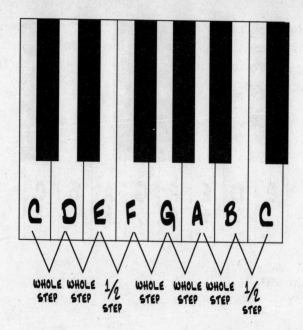

Now let's take it a step further. Instead of using the letter names for each note in the C major scale (like C, D, E, F, G, A, B, C), let's give them numbers instead, starting on the number 1. Now you can call the notes 1, 2, 3, 4, 5, 6, 7, 8.

Don't let that confuse you . . . we're just calling the notes in the scale by numbers rather than their letter names.

The reason we want to number the scale steps is because it helps explain the way to name intervals larger than half steps. A whole step (2 half steps) is sometimes called the interval of a second.

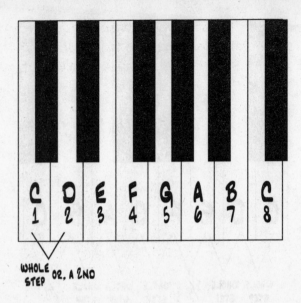

WHOLE STEP OR, A 2ND

Why? Because we went up to the second note in the major scale.

The names of the intervals continue in this order: third, fourth, fifth, sixth, and seventh. The interval of an eighth is called an octave. See how they follow the numbers we gave the notes in the major scale?

When counting keys to figure out an interval on the keyboard, be sure that you count the key that you are starting on as key #1 and figure out the major scale that starts on that key. Then, figure out what number in the scale corresponds with the other note, and that's your interval.

For example, the interval between C and F would be the interval of a fourth because, starting on C, the F is number 4 in the major scale that starts on C.

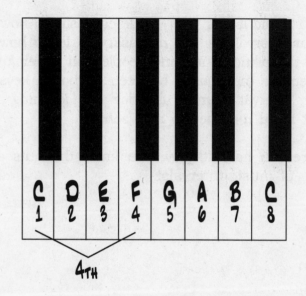

As another example, the interval between C and A would be the interval of a sixth because, starting on C, the A is number 6 in the major scale starting on C.

Intervals can be heard in music, as well as being seen on the keyboard. In addition, knowing intervals can really help in figuring our chord symbols (which we'll be getting to very soon).

Some kids get very good at recognizing the sounds of different intervals just by listening to them in the melodies of the songs that they are learning.

For example, in the melody to "Here Comes the Bride" (which on a keyboard is C, F, F, F), the interval between "Here" and "Comes" is a good example of a fourth.

Don't panic if this was a little confusing. Knowing about intervals is not necessary to learn how to play the piano. But some people find it helpful to remember the spaces between keyboard keys in their interval names as they are learning the right hand melodies to new songs.

There you have it! Now you know the nuts and bolts of music intervals!

"Nuts & Bolts" for Chapter 3

If you are someone who likes math, you might be interested in knowing that the beat values of music notes are all based on fractions. As a matter of fact, that's where the names of the notes came from—from the fractional values of the notes. If you can remember the fractions, you will always know both the names of the notes and how many beats they are worth.

So, all of you math geniuses, get ready!

Start with a whole note, which equals 4 beats. Half of a whole note is a half note, which equals 2 beats. A quarter of a whole note is a quarter note, which equals 1 beat. An eighth of a whole note is an eighth note, which equals ½ beat.

Did you notice that the fraction used to divide the whole note is the name of the new note (a whole note divided by a half equals a half note and so forth)? Also, dividing the 4 beats of the whole note by the fraction that matches the name of the new note will give you the number of beats that the new note is worth.

For example, if you divide 4 beats by a quarter, the answer is 1 beat, which is the number of beats that each quarter note is worth. Don't forget that if there is a dot after any of these notes, it increases the note's value by a half again as much as its normal value.

It is important to point out that in nonclassical-style piano playing, *note values do not have to be played exactly as they are written.* If you play things exactly as they are written, it will tend to sound very robotic and machinelike.

But when they are first learning a song, some kids find it helpful to say the names of the notes to themselves so that they can play the rhythm of a song as it is written. Then, as they get to know the song better, the rhythm can be "loosened up" and played the way that someone would sing or whistle the song.

There you have it! Now you know the nuts and bolts of rhythm in music!

"Nuts & Bolts" for Chapter 4

Now you know the basics of reading music notes in the treble clef staff!

Every once in a while, you may run across a few other music signs that will give you some extra directions on how to play the melody.

Here are explanations for a few of them:

A curved line over several notes is called a slur. It means to play these notes very smoothly. This style of playing is called *legato*.

Notes that have a dot above or below them should be played as short as possible. This style of playing is called *staccato*.

Notes that have a sideways "V" sign above them should be played as loudly as possible. This sign is called an *accent sign*.

Notes that have a sign above them that looks like a "bird's eye" (a half circle with a dot under it) should be held for longer than their normal beat value. It is up to the person playing how many beats to give these notes. This sign is called a *fermata*. Many people simply call it a "hold" sign.

Sometimes, you might see a fancy letter "f" or a fancy letter "p" either above or below the notes. These are signs that tell you when to play loud or soft.

The "f" stands for the Italian word *forte,* which means loud. The "p" stands for the Italian word *piano,* which means soft.

Did you know that when the piano was invented in the 1700s, it was originally called the *pianoforte?*

It was called the pianoforte because it was the first keyboard instrument that was able to control the volume by how hard or how softly a person pressed the keys down. Other keyboard instruments back in those days were able to control their volume only with foot pedals.

The inventor of the piano, Bartolomeo Cristofori, was an Italian man. That's probably why so many of the directions in music are given in the Italian language rather than in English. Some of the other terms that we have learned in this section are also Italian, such as *legato* and *staccato.*

Additional Italian musical terms may be found in some dictionaries. Small, inexpensive dictionaries of music may be purchased, if you are interested, and they can come in very handy. You can go to our website at www .scottthepianoguy.com for more information.

However, never lose sight of the fact that your ear should be the final judge. If it sounds good to the person playing it, *that's what matters.* The only purpose of the notation is to act as a guide if you need it.

There you have it! Now you know the nuts and bolts of traditional musical directions!

"Nuts & Bolts" for Chapter 5

Some kids like to know how to make chords without looking at the chord charts.

Because the distance between notes in chords can be measured in half steps, that is another way to figure out the notes in a chord you might not know yet. Remember from our earlier discussion of intervals that the closest distance between two keys with no other keys in between them is one half step. For example, from the C key to the C sharp key is one half step.

In order to build a chord, all you need to know is:

1. How many notes are in that particular chord
2. How many half steps are in between each note

Below is a chart that shows you:

- the different types of chords
- the number of notes in each chord
- the distance in half steps between each of those notes, and
- an example of each type of chord built on C as the root note

CHORD TYPE	NUMBER OF NOTES	DISTANCE BETWEEN NOTES (IN HALF STEPS, R=ROOT)	EXAMPLE SYMBOL & NOTES USING C AS THE ROOT	
MAJOR	3	R-4-3	C	C-E-G
MINOR	3	R-3-4	CMIN	C-E♭-G
SEVENTH	4	R-4-3-3	C7	C-E-G-B♭
MAJOR SEVENTH	4	R-4-3-4	CMAJ7	C-E-G-B
MINOR SEVENTH	4	R-3-4-3	CMIN7	C-E♭-G-B♭
AUGMENTED	3	R-4-4	CAUG	C-E-G♯
DIMINISHED	3	R-3-3	CDIM	C-E♭-G♭

Let's try building a C major chord to test it out.

Look at the chart, and you will see that a major chord should have 3 notes, with the distance in between notes being root, up 4 half steps, and up 3 more half steps.

So, to make a C major chord, here are the steps that you should follow:

- Start on the root, which is C.
- Go up 4 half-steps to E.
- Go up 3 more half-steps to G.

It works, doesn't it? Let's try another one . . .

How about an F major chord? The steps are

- Start on the root, which is F.
- Go up four half steps to A.
- Go up three more half steps to C.

It's easier than you thought, isn't it?

Now let's try a G7 chord so that you have a chance to build a different type of chord.

First, check the chart. You will see that seventh chords have four notes, with the distance in between notes being root, up four half-steps, then up three half steps, and then up three more half-steps.

- Start on the root, which is G.
- Go up four half steps to B.
- Go up three half steps to D.
- Go up three more half steps to F.

That makes the notes in a G7 chord: G, B, D, F.

As you are learning new chords when you play different songs, it is completely up to you whether you figure out your chords using half steps or using individual chord charts.

But just in case you get to some chord symbol that you might not have a chord chart for, now you can figure it out by counting half-steps.

There you have it! Now you know the nuts and bolts of making chords!

"Nuts & Bolts" for Chapter 6

Sometimes when you are learning a new song, you may have a little trouble getting the rhythm of the melody to come out right. If this happens to you, it may help to know something called the *time signature* of the song so that you can figure out the rhythm by counting out the beats in each measure.

At the beginning of any song, there will always be two numbers, one above the other one. These numbers are called the time signature. Each number stands for something different.

The top number of the time signature tells us how many beats are in each measure of the song. This means that the notes and rests in every single measure of that song must add up to that particular number. The most common numbers found on the top of the time signature are 2, 3, or 4. For example, if the top number of the time signature is 4, then the notes and rests in each measure of that song must add up to 4 beats. Another way of saying this is that the notes and rests are "measured" into groups of 4 beats each—that's why the sections of notes and rests are called *measures*.

The bottom number of the time signature tells us what kind of note will get 1 beat in that particular song.

"But doesn't the quarter note always get 1 beat?" you might ask.

The answer is: "Yes, most of the time, but not always."

Here's how you can tell. Pretend that the bottom number of the time signature is the denominator (the bottom number) of a fraction. Make the numerator (the top number) of the fraction the number 1. The resulting fraction will then tell you what kind of note will be getting one beat in that song.

For example, the bottom number of the time signature in all of the songs that we have played so far has been 4. If you pretend that 4 is the denominator of a fraction and that the numerator is 1, you will have the fraction ¼. This would mean that the quarter note would be getting 1 beat in any song that has the number 4 as the bottom number of its time signature. The number 4 is the most common number found as the bottom number of time signatures, but it is not the only one that you will ever see.

Assuming that the bottom number of the time signature in most of your songs will be the number 4, you will usually only need to check the top number of the time signature to find out how many beats there will be in each measure of the song that you are playing.

Also, don't forget that in this style of nonclassical playing it is more important to play something that sounds good than to play something exactly as it is notated.

The music notation for the melody line and its rhythm is just a guide that you can feel free to change a little bit to the way you like it to sound.

Trust your ears!

If it sounds good, it is good!

There you have it! Now you know the nuts and bolts of time signatures!

"Nuts & Bolts" for Chapter 8

Inversions are another way to make the chords that you play sound different. Chord inversions are the "rearranging" or "restacking" of the notes of a chord into a different order.

We have been working with mostly three note chords in their root positions. This means we have formed the chord with the root in the bottom or lowest position.

For example: C major has been formed with the notes C, E, G, and A major is A, C#, E . . . and so forth. The root note, which is also the note that names the chord, is the lowest note of the chord. Now, to add some "color" to your playing, we will try some chord inversions!

Let's invert the C major chord, which simply means to restack the notes of the chord in an order other than in the root position. An easy way to invert the C major chord (C, E, G) is to think of playing "leapfrog" with the notes.

Start with the lowest note, C, and have it jump over the E and G notes. Now the C major chord is inverted (E, G, C). Notice that all we did is play the chord with the notes in a different order. Again, this is known as an inversion—simply stacking the notes of the chord in an order other than root position. If you want, you can restack them again by letting the E leapfrog over the G and C. The C major chord in this inversion would be G, C, E.

C Major Chord Inversions

The first and fourth shown are in root position (one octave apart).
The two middle ones are inversions.

You will find that the different arrangements of notes within the chords gives new sounds to your playing even though they are the same chords.

It is your decision as a nonclassical piano player to play a chord either in root position or in an inversion whenever you want to. Let your ears be the judge!

Some good advice is to usually play a chord in root position, but every now and then throw in an inversion just to keep things interesting!

There you have it! Now you know the nuts and bolts of chord inversions!

MAJOR CHORDS

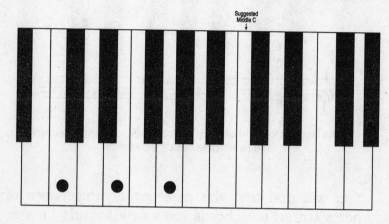

C

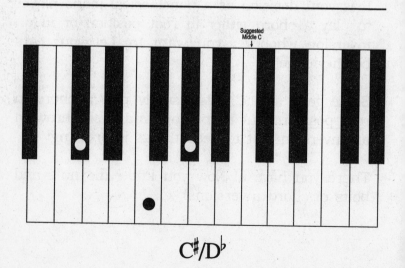

C#/D♭

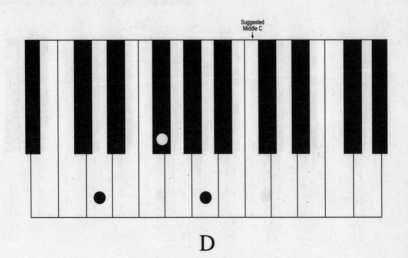

D

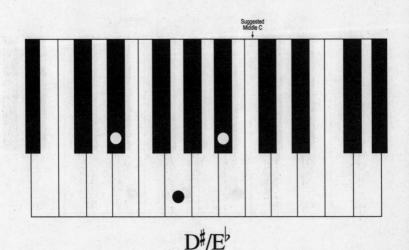

D#/E♭

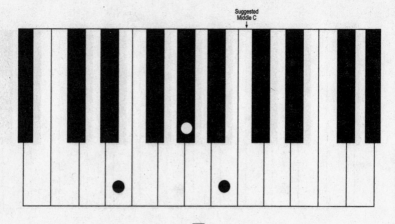

E

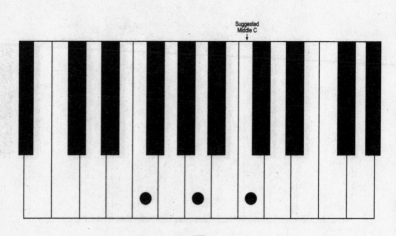

F

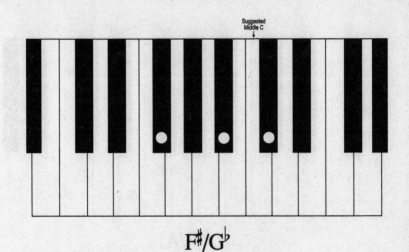

$F^{\sharp}/G^{\flat}$

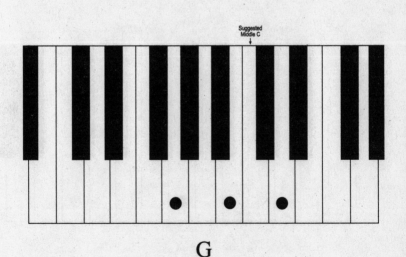

G

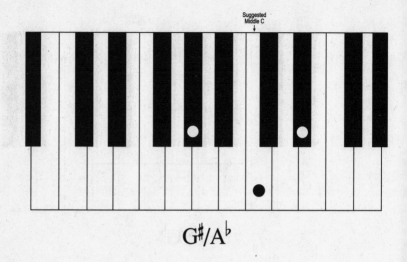

G#/A♭

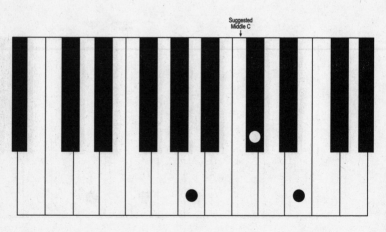

A

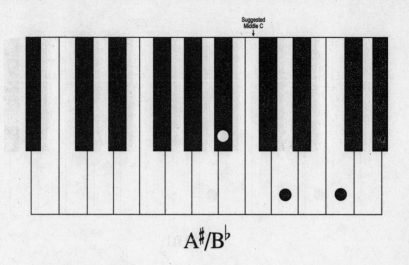

A♯/B♭

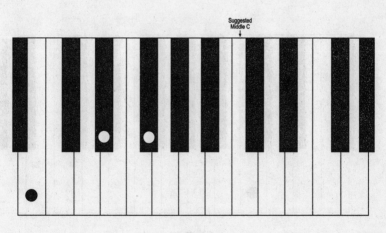

B

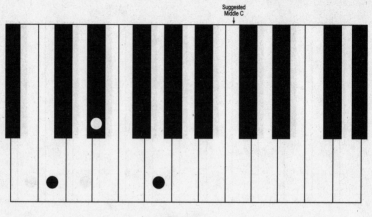

Cmin

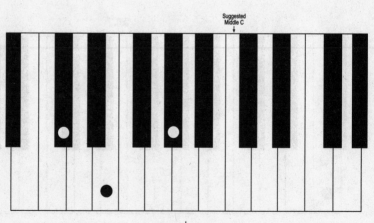

C#/D♭ min

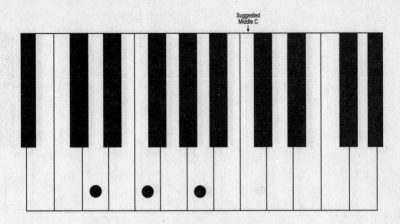

D min

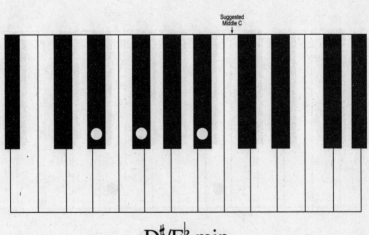

D#/E♭ min

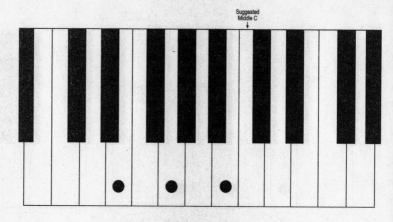

E min

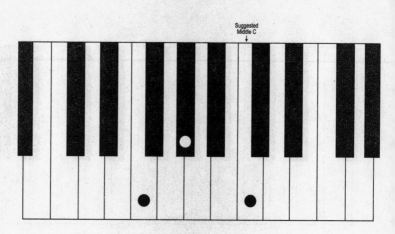

F min

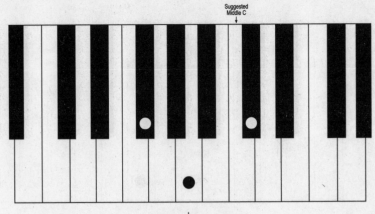

F#/G♭ min

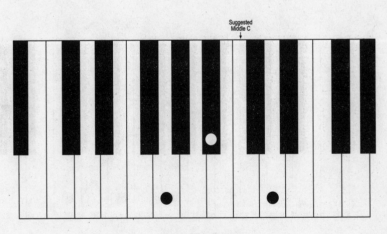

G min

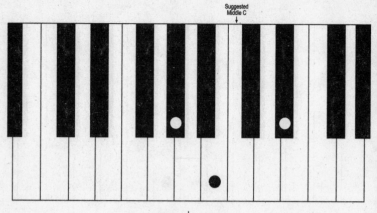

G#/A♭ min

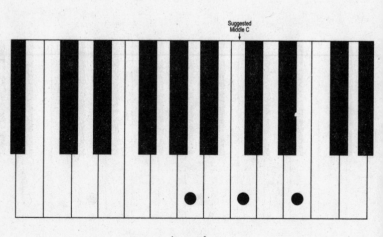

A min

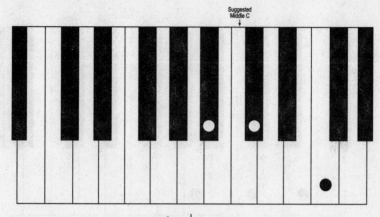

A#/B♭ min

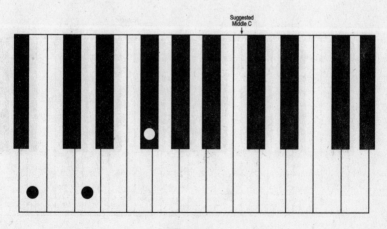

B min

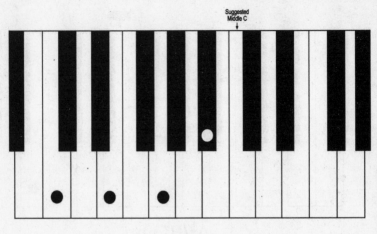

C7

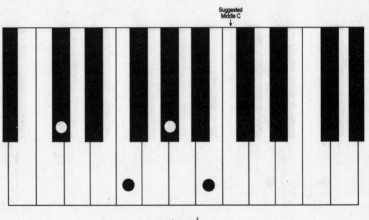

C♯/D♭7

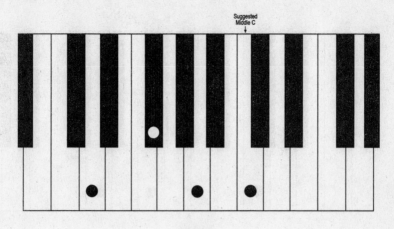

D7

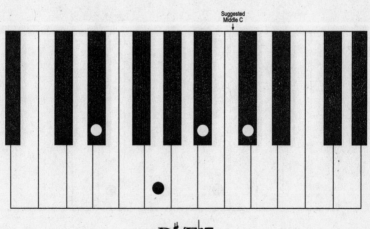

D#/E♭7

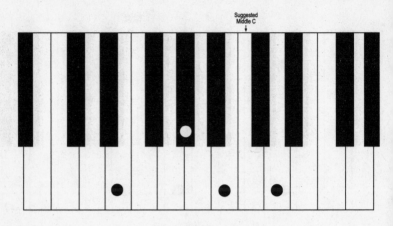

E7

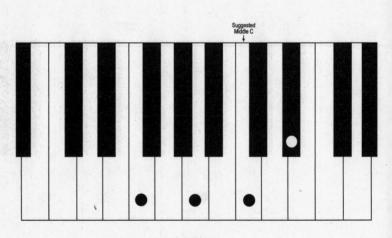

F7

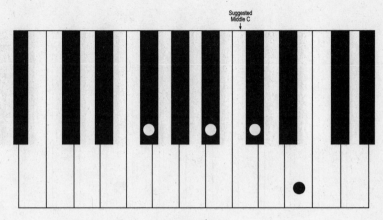

F#/G♭7

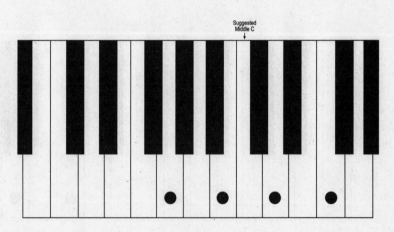

G7

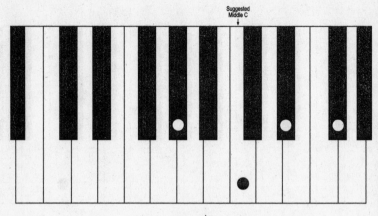

G♯/A♭7

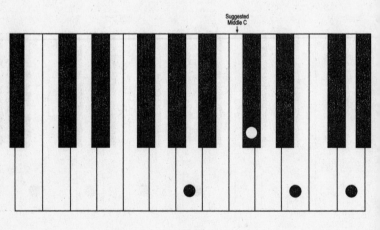

A7

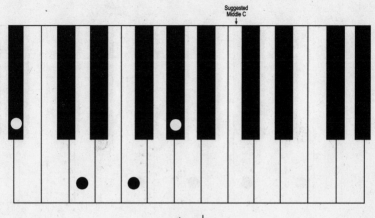

A#/B♭7

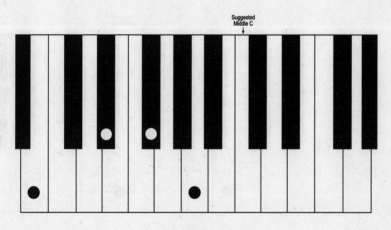

B7

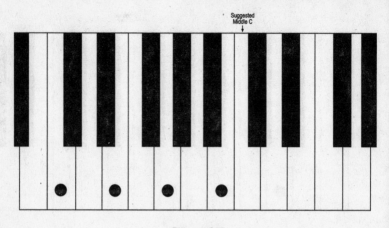

Cmaj7

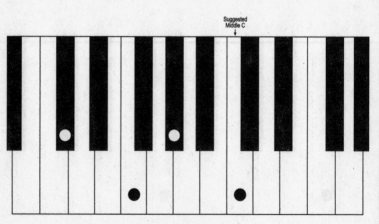

C#/D♭maj7

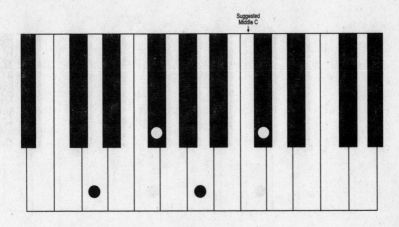

Dmaj7

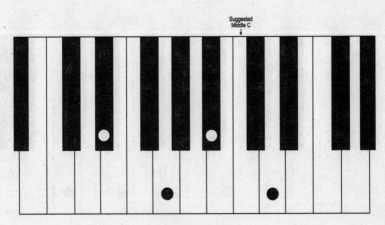

D#/E♭maj7

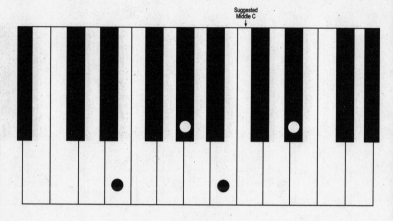

Emaj7

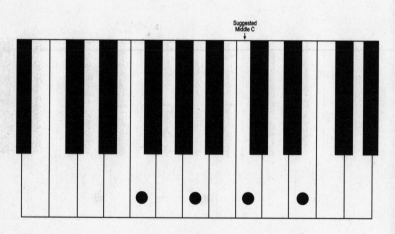

Fmaj7

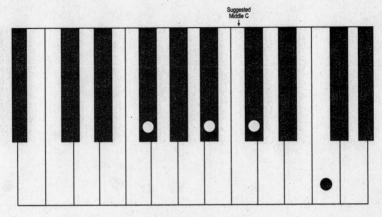

F#/G♭maj7

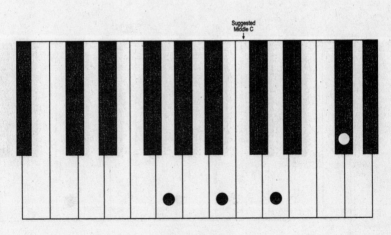

Gmaj7

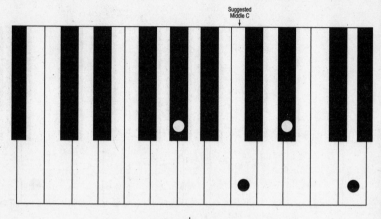

$G^{\#}/A^{\flat}maj7$

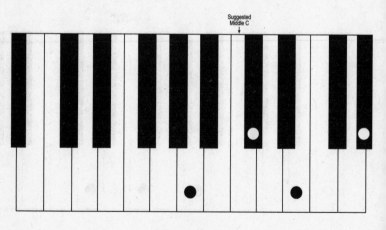

Amaj7

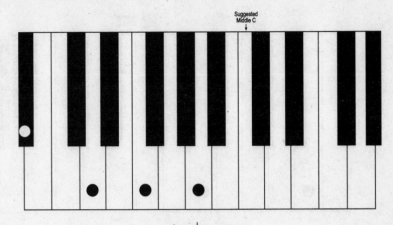

A♯/B♭maj7

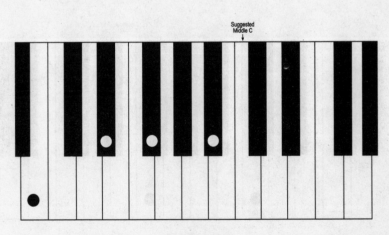

Bmaj7

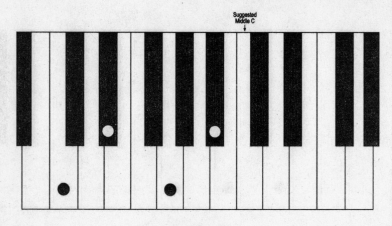

Cmin7

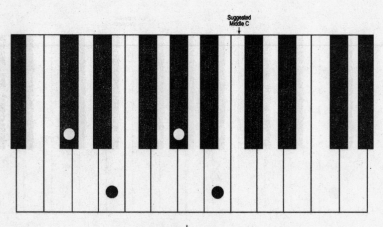

C#/D♭min7

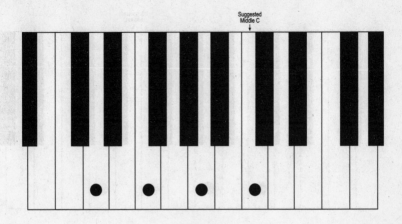

Dmin7

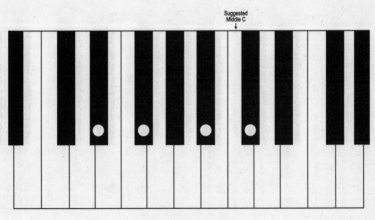

D#/E♭min7

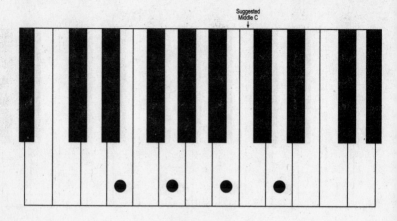

Emin7

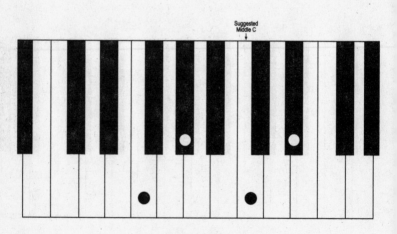

Fmin7

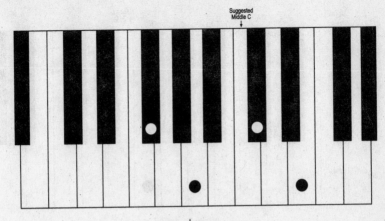

F#/G♭min7

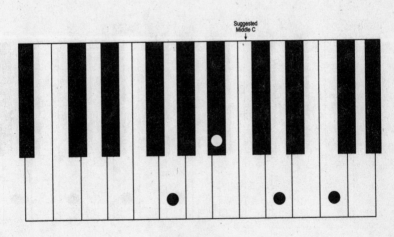

Gmin7

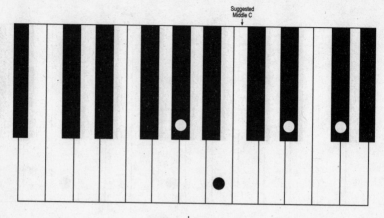

G#/A♭min7

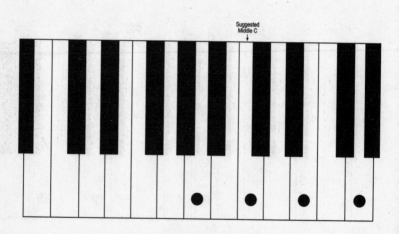

Amin7

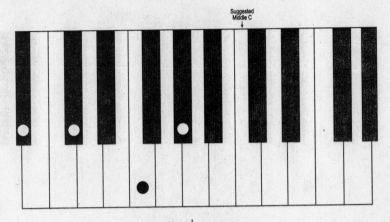

A♯/B♭min7

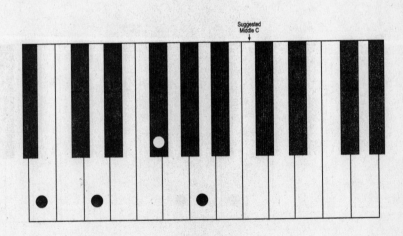

Bmin7

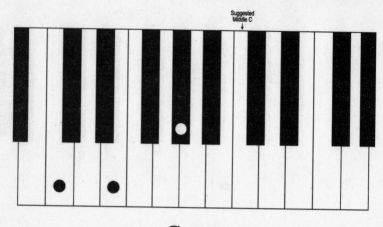

C aug

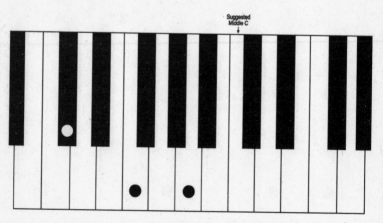

C♯/D♭ aug

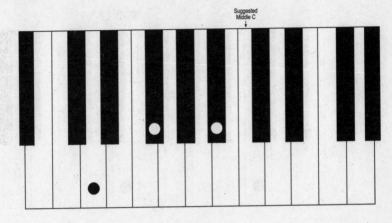

D aug

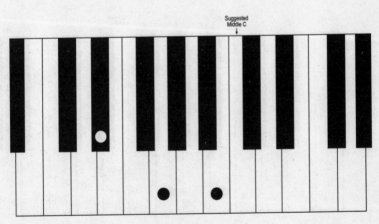

D#/E♭ aug

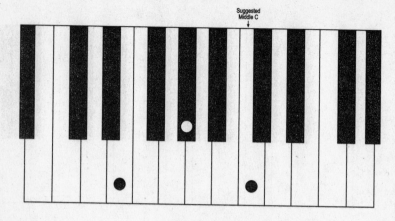

E aug

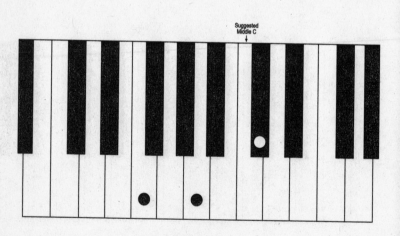

F aug

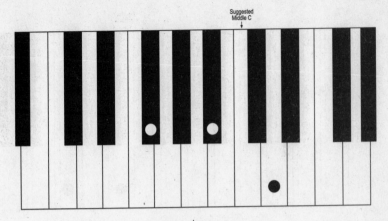

F#/G♭ aug

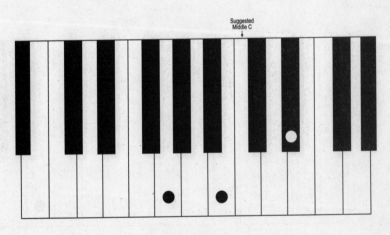

G aug

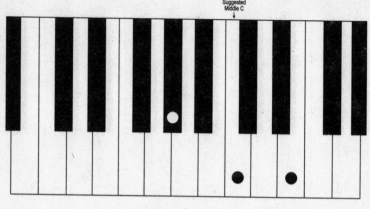

G#/A♭ aug

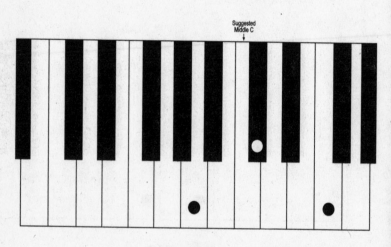

A aug

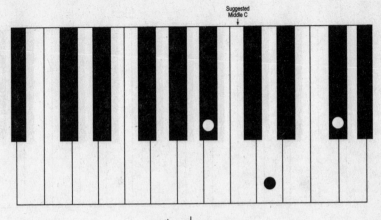

A♯/B♭ aug

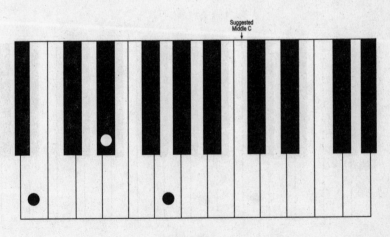

B aug

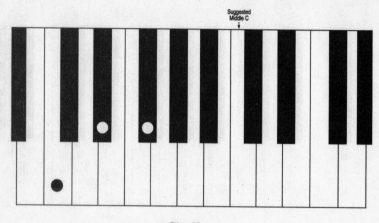

C dim

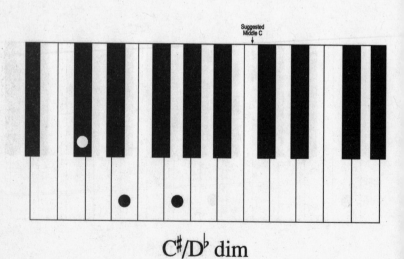

C#/D♭ dim

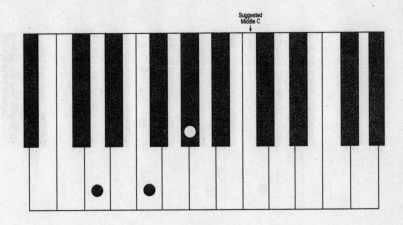

D dim

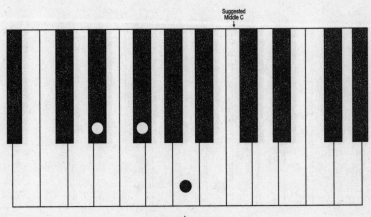

D$^\sharp$/E$^\flat$ dim

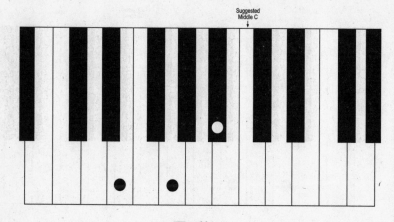

E dim

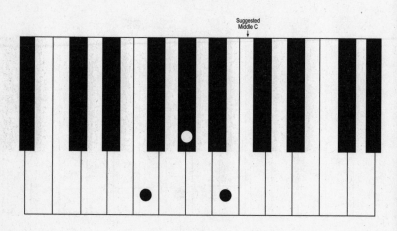

F dim

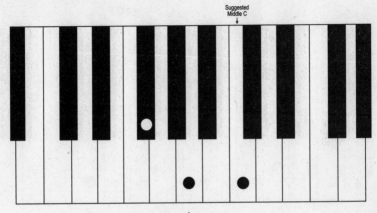

F#/G♭ dim

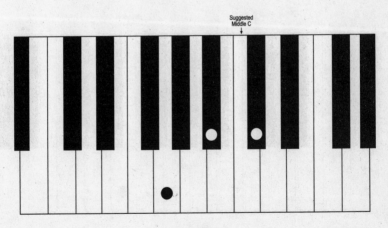

G dim

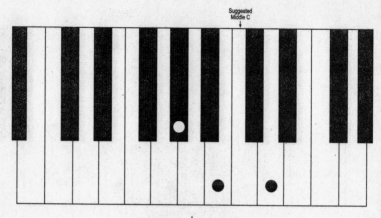

G#/A♭ dim

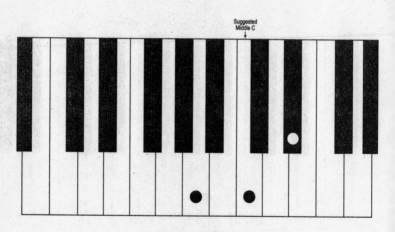

A dim

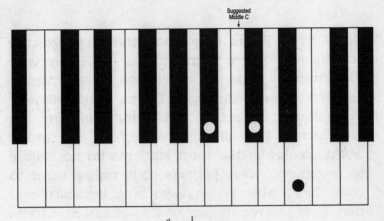

A♯/B♭ dim

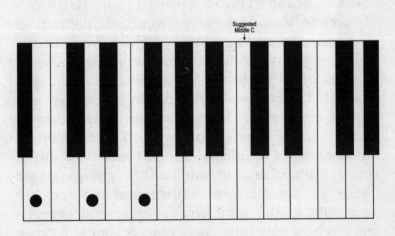

B dim

Scott "The Piano Guy" Houston's background combines a degree from Indiana University with over twenty years of experience in the music industry. From teaching to playing professionally to managing a music publishing company, he has been a part of many aspects of the music world. Realizing that most students do not aspire to become concert pianists, but rather want to enjoy being able to sit down at a keyboard and play their favorite music, he has taught hundreds of thousands of students successfully nationwide at universities, colleges, and through his public television series and specials.

Susan Stone Tidrow received her Bachelor's Degree in Music Education from the University of Indianapolis and graduate degrees from Butler University and Indiana University. Her passion for performance-based music education led her to install thirty-two keyboards in her elementary music classroom. During her thirty-plus years in teaching, she has given keyboard instruction to thousands of students as part of their music class curriculum, in addition to giving private lessons. She has also written and directed her students in the performance of several elementary school musicals each year. Susan still "goes to school" every day at Mary Castle Elementary School in Indianapolis, Indiana.